IMAGES
of America

MONO LAKE
BASIN

Near the west shore of Mono Lake, Lee Vining is at the junction of Highway 395 (which runs along the eastern base of the Sierra Nevada) and Highway 120, the route over Tioga Pass to Yosemite National Park. The scenic inland sea is extremely alkaline and two-and-a-half times as salty as the ocean, with a unique ecosystem of algae and invertebrates that supports millions of birds. The boundary between the mountains and the Great Basin desert makes for a unique blend of life in a striking setting. (Courtesy of Don Banta.)

ON THE COVER: Boat tours from the Mono Inn visited the islands of Mono Lake and the California gull nesting colony on Negit Island through the 1930s. This Frashers Foto photograph was taken in 1930. (Courtesy of Frashers Foto Collection.)

IMAGES
of America

MONO LAKE
BASIN

David Carle and Don Banta

ARCADIA
PUBLISHING

Published by Arcadia Publishing
Charleston, South Carolina

Library of Congress Catalog Card Number: 2008926274

For all general information contact Arcadia Publishing at:
Telephone 843-853-2070
Fax 843-853-0044
E-mail sales@arcadiapublishing.com
For customer service and orders:
Toll-Free 1-888-313-2665

Visit us on the Internet at www.arcadiapublishing.com

This book is for the past, present, and future residents of the Mono Lake Basin and for the travelers to the region.

CONTENTS

ACKNOWLEDGMENTS

For their help in gathering photographs and material for this book, we would like to thank Arya Degenhardt, Elin Ljung, and Greg Reis of the Mono Lake Committee; Jon Kazmierski with the U.S. Forest Service; Inyo National Forest; Norman DeChambeau and the Mono Basin Historical Society; Ilene Mandelbaum; Linda LaPierre; and Bud, Tracy, and Scott Hayward. Certain images in this volume appear courtesy of the Mono Basin Historical Society (MBHS), the Frashers Fotos Collection (FFC), the U.S. Forest Service, Inyo National Forest (USFS/INF), the Mono Lake Tufa State Reserve, California State Parks (MLTSR), the Mono Lake Committee (MLC), Robert Lewis (RL), Ruby Nay Etchemendy (RNE), Vance B. Rhudy (VBR), and William C. Hayward (WH). Unless otherwise noted, other photographs are provided by Don Banta.

INTRODUCTION

Mono Lake, an inland sea that is at least 760,000 years old, dominates the landscape east of the Sierra Nevada crest between Yosemite National Park and the Nevada border. The lake's strange water chemistry, twice as salty as the ocean and as alkaline as dish detergent, produces limestone tufa towers where freshwater springs emerge from the lake bottom. Though Mono Lake has been described as "California's Dead Sea," it actually teems with life and is one of the world's most biologically productive lake ecosystems. Algae are food for brine shrimp and alkali flies that in turn feed millions of migratory and nesting birds. Volcanoes form three sides of the basin and also the islands within the lake. The wall of the Sierra Nevada defines the western boundary of the Mono Basin with peaks over 13,000 feet.

The Kuzedika, or Mono Lake Paiute Indians, moved up to the mountain meadows west of Mono Lake each summer and often crossed over to Yosemite. They survived challenging winters on the east side of the high-altitude lake basin. In the summer of 1852, soldiers chasing Chief Tenaya from Yosemite Valley followed his route into the Mono Lake Basin. Lt. Tredwell Moore's expedition never located Tenaya but did discover signs of gold-bearing quartz. The reports from this expedition led miner Leroy Vining and his brother, Richard, to the Mono Basin in 1853. They established a sawmill at the mouth of a canyon beside the creek that would become known as Lee Vining Creek, and Leroy's name would ultimately be given to the town, Lee Vining, that was established nearby. Gold was first mined along the northern edge of the Mono Lake Basin at Mono Diggings (just east of Conway Summit), but mining also developed in Lundy Canyon (the Homer Mining District), at Bennettville in the Tioga Canyon, and west of Lee Vining on the hills overlooking the lake (Log Cabin Mine). The greatest mining success in the region occurred just north of the Mono Basin at Bodie, which had its peak (nearly 10,000 residents) between 1879 and 1881.

Settlers established ranches and farms to serve those mining towns, especially Bodie, with food and fiber products. Agricultural family names included Conway, DeChambeau, Farrington, Mattly, Nay, Sylvester, Thompson, and the McPhersons (who had a ranch on Paoha Island in the middle of Mono Lake). They raised livestock and grew vegetable crops, battling the basin's challenging short growing season. Potatoes were one of the most reliable crops, along with hay or alfalfa to feed dairy and meat animals.

The piñon-juniper forests and Jeffrey and lodgepole pines on surrounding hills furnished firewood and lumber for the mines and towns. Mono Mills, south of the lake, processed much of that timber, which reached Bodie via steam vessels that crossed the lake then transferred their loads onto wagons. After 1882, the Bodie-to-Benton railroad followed the east shore of Mono Lake from Mono Mills to the mining town. In time, the Mono National Forest (later merged into the Inyo National Forest) was established to manage timber, grazing, and recreational uses. The resource-extraction era included speculation and excitement attending oil drilling on Paoha Island. Hydroelectric power plants were also established within the watershed at Lundy Canyon, Lee Vining Canyon, and the June Lake Loop, served by reservoirs constructed higher in the watershed.

The base of the Sierra Nevada has always served as a north-south travel corridor, and the nearby passes funneled travelers over the mountains. The town of Lee Vining was founded in 1926, and grocery stores, gas stations, garages, motels, restaurants, and bars have served travelers as well as residents ever since. A road was pushed over Tioga Pass at 9,943 feet above sea level, connecting the Mono Lake Basin with Yosemite National Park. The late-spring opening and winter closures of the highway have controlled the seasonal influx of tourists and travelers ever since. Opening of the pass was celebrated each year up to World War II with a community fish fry. Another annual community celebration was begun by the Mono Inn on the west shore of Mono Lake north of Lee Vining; the Mark Twain Days celebration drew hundreds of people in the 1920s and 1930s to watch speedboat races, bathing beauty contests, baseball games, and other events. (Mark Twain wrote about his 1862 visit to Mono Lake in his book *Roughing It*.)

The June Lake Loop occupies the southwestern portion of the Mono Lake watershed, where four lakes are connected by creeks that ultimately send water to Mono Lake. Carson Camp was the first resort and pack station operating on the loop. The Hollywood crowd started visiting in the 1920s. Fishing was the big attraction, and the lakes and streams became fabled for their cutthroat, brown, and rainbow trout. The Fish and Game Department established the Fern Creek fish hatchery in 1926 and planted fish into Eastern Sierra lakes and streams that had historically been without trout.

Mountain winters above 6,500 feet in elevation bring challenges and special opportunities for residents and visitors. Keeping roads plowed when major blizzards hit is one challenge. In 1938 and 1939, primitive rope tows run by ski clubs began to appear, operating free to skiers (at first), on the slopes of Conway Summit, on the hill behind Lee Vining, near Oh! Ridge (approaching June Lake), on the Aeolian Buttes above West Portal, and other places. The June Mountain Ski Area was established in 1961.

West Portal was one of four construction camps where laborers employed by the Los Angeles Department of Water and Power worked from 1934 to 1941 on a system to tap four of Mono Lake's tributary streams. Those construction years were like a wild-west boom era for Lee Vining and June Lake. Things quieted down in the following decades, but the impacts of diversions on Mono Lake gradually became apparent. The Mono Lake Committee was established in 1978 to save the lake's ecosystem from the effects of increasing salinity. The committee partnered with the National Audubon Society and CalTrout in 16 years of court battles. In 1994, the Los Angeles Department of Water and Power's water licenses were amended by the state to reduce diversions and restore both the lake and the dried-up creeks. That environmental victory brought national and international recognition to the region.

One

FORMING THE WATERSHED

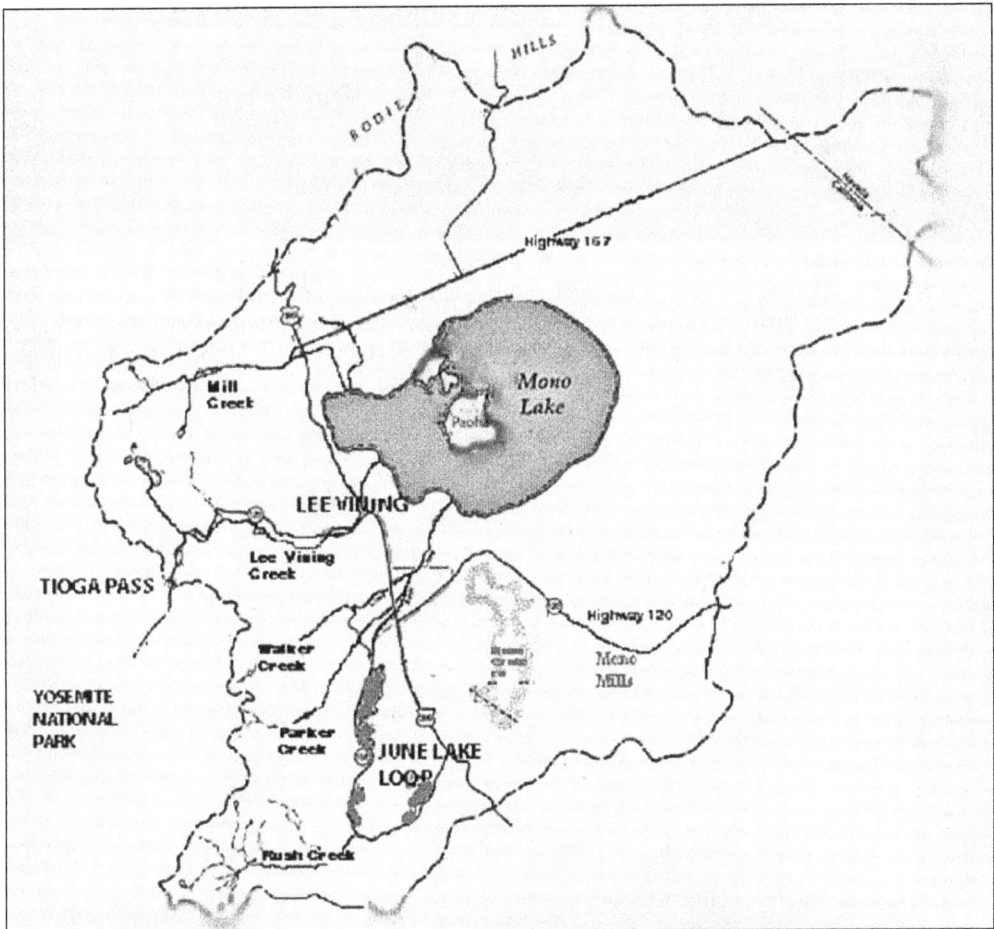

The Mono Basin Watershed map shows the lake's primary tributaries: Lee Vining Creek (from Tioga Canyon), Mill Creek (from Lundy Canyon), and Rush Creek (from the June Lake Loop). Walker and Parker Creeks drain into Rush Creek east of Highway 395. The town of Lee Vining is at the Junction of Highway 395 and Highway 120 (the Tioga Pass road that leads to Yosemite National Park). (Redrawn from a MLC map.)

Mono Lake dominates the view to the east from the crest of the Sierra Nevada. It is a vast inland sea with salty, alkaline water that produces a unique ecosystem and photogenic limestone tufa towers. The lake is surrounded on three sides by volcanic hills and contains very young volcanic islands. The east face of the Sierra Nevada forms the western boundary of the basin, with peaks along its crest over 13,000 feet tall. In this image, Black Point, a volcanic cinder cone, is to the left

(north) of the lake. The largest island is Paoha, farther left is Negit Island, and the small Gaines Island between Negit and Black Point is the remnant of a land bridge that formed in 1979 as the lake dropped due to diversions. The recovering lake has risen high enough here to stop coyotes from crossing the land bridge to the gull breeding colony on Negit. (Courtesy of USFS/INF.)

Rush Creek is the largest of five major tributaries to Mono Lake. Fish and game biologist Eldon Vestal took this photograph in the early 1940s, before Rush Creek water was diverted to Los Angeles and the lake had declined. At the far left, a diversion channel takes water toward one of four ponds created by rancher Walt Dombrowski to attract waterfowl. Runoff from the Eastern Sierra Nevada snowpack replaces about 3 feet of water lost from the lake to evaporation each year. (Courtesy of the MLTSR.)

The Grant Lake Reservoir (left) passes water from the June Lake Loop down Rush Creek toward Mono Lake and also sends water into the Los Angeles aqueduct system. The June Lake Loop occupies the southwestern portion of the Mono Lake Basin. The area has been called Horseshoe Canyon, because a Pleistocene Era glacier carved a crescent-shaped path that wrapped around Reverse Peak (where this photograph was taken). June and Gull Lakes are connected by Reverse Creek, named because the creek travels toward the Sierra crest, rather than away, unlike most streams flowing out of the mountains. Reverse Creek drains into Silver Lake, which also receives water from upper Rush Creek. (Photograph by David Carle.)

Mono Lake's strange water forms suds when agitated by the wind. It contains three primary salts: carbonates, chlorides, and sulfates. Adding baking soda, table salt, and Epsom salts to fresh water in the correct proportions can approximate the unique lake water chemistry, which, at pH 10, is as alkaline as some detergents. (Courtesy of the MLTSR.)

Swimmers bob on the surface of Mono Lake, kept from sinking by the concentration of dissolved particles. The water stings eyes, but washing away the salts leaves skin clean and soft. Mono Lake became salty because its basin has no outlet. For over 760,000 years, the lake has been accumulating minerals washed in by creeks and deposited directly into it as volcanic ash. (Courtesy of the MLC.)

Volcanoes, including the Mono Craters south of the lake, form three sides of the Mono Basin's boundaries. The islands within the lake also have volcanic origins. Eruptions contributed ash to the surrounding landscape and into the lake itself, influencing the unique mix of minerals in Mono Lake. The basin, however, is not a caldera. The Sierra Nevada forms its western wall and is not of volcanic origin. (Photograph by David Carle.)

There were two crater lakes on the east side of Paoha Island in 1930. The lake on the left was called Heart Lake, and the other was Red Lake. When the lake level dropped following stream diversions that began in 1941, both craters dried up. Paoha, the white island, formed only about 350 years ago. Most of the whitish land of Paoha is lake-bottom mud that was lifted above the surface by magma from below. (Courtesy of FFC.)

THE MONO BASIN IN QUATERNARY TIME.
Scale 1:250,000.

The ice-age lake that filled the basin 700 feet deeper than today is called Lake Russell to honor the scientist Israel Russell, who studied the Mono Lake Basin in the 1880s. Russell named the Mono Craters and Negit and Paoha Islands. He chose Paiute words for the islands, *Negit* meaning "blue-winged goose" (perhaps a reference to the gulls that nest on the island) and *Paoha* referring to water spirits that in Paiute legend occupy the steamy hot springs on the island. Superimposed on Russell's map of the ice-age lake is an outline of Mono Lake as it appeared in 1941, the year stream diversions began to Los Angeles. Note the glaciers that extended all the way to the lakeshore; icebergs must have floated in the lake in those years. (Redrawn from Russell, 1889.)

One of Israel Russell's crew, Willard D. Johnson, chiseled a lake-elevation benchmark on Negit Island on November 5, 1883: an upside-down *T* with a 4-inch horizontal line at the water line and a 10-inch vertical line. In the late 1950s, Don Banta (right) went with Hugh Knox (seated), S. T. Harding, and Harding's grandson (left) to Negit Island and relocated Russell's benchmark. Harding's cane in this photograph is to the left of the vertical line; Knox is looking at the location (a small arrow has been added to the image). Mono Lake was at 6,411 feet above sea level in 1883 (higher than Russell had estimated). Through most of the decades that followed, the lake covered the mark. Sometime prior to 1950, Wallace McPherson spotted the submerged mark from his boat. After 1950, it became exposed again as the lake continued dropping due to stream diversions.

Two

THE NATURAL HISTORY OF MONO LAKE

Few things can live in Mono Lake's harsh alkaline water, but those species thrive in incredible abundance. Trillions of brine shrimp unique to Mono Lake (*Artemia monica*) feed on microscopic algae and diatoms. This is a female; note the dark egg sack at the base of her tail. (Courtesy of the MLTSR.)

The brine shrimp crowd the water during the summer months, above. Adult shrimp die before each autumn but lay eggs that settle as cysts onto the lake bottom and hatch in the spring. Below, the edges of the lake and tufa towers emerging from the water are crowded with alkali flies during the summer. Adult flies crawl into the water to lay eggs. Larvae feed on algae on the submerged rocks and eventually form dark pupae cases. Adult flies do their best to avoid people, so there is no need to consider them a pest. Both flies and shrimp serve as nutritious food sources for birds. (Above, courtesy of the MLTSR; below, courtesy of the MLC.)

The enormous quantities of shrimp and flies feed over a million birds at Mono Lake each year. Two species of phalaropes, totaling at least 150,000 of the small shorebirds, use the lake as a fueling stop during their long southward migrations. Red-necked (*Phalaropus lobatus*) and Wilson's phalaropes (*Phalaropus tricolor*) nest far north of here (some above the arctic circle) but spend winter far to the south, in Chile and Argentina. Mono Lake is a critically important resting and refueling point for these birds, which are often seen in large flocks that turn in acrobatic unison above the water. (Both, courtesy of the MLTSR.)

Over one million eared grebes (*Podiceps negricollis*) come to Mono Lake each autumn after they finish nesting in the north. They usually stay at the lake until the first winter storms bring an end to the availability of shrimp and fly food, then the grebes fly south to the Salton Sea and the Gulf of California to spend the winter. They are diving birds, with legs set far back on their bodies to propel them efficiently underwater but not positioned to support them well on land. Perhaps a quarter of the world's population of eared grebes is on Mono Lake each year. (Above, courtesy of the MLC; below, photograph by David Carle.)

Most of the California gulls (*Larus californicus*) found in this state are born at Mono Lake. (There are many other types of gulls in California.) About 50,000 adult gulls return each spring from the coast to crowd onto Mono Lake's islands, lay eggs in simple nest scrapes on the ground, and raise about 30,000 chicks in good years with the abundant food found at the lake. By September, the gulls and their offspring fly back across the mountains to spend the winter along the coast, from Northern California down to Baja California in Mexico. Negit Island was the primary nesting island until the dropping lake connected it to shore in 1979. Though the land bridge that allowed coyotes onto Negit is now back underwater, most nesting was still occurring on the smaller islets as of 2008. (Both, courtesy of the MLC.)

Tufa towers form beneath the surface of the lake, where freshwater springs deliver calcium to mix with the carbonate-rich lake water forming calcium carbonate (limestone). Since they form underwater, those towers visible onshore or rising above the surface are signs that the lake level dropped. This photograph was taken in the state reserve below the Mono Lake County Park on the northwest shore of Mono Lake. (Photograph by Betty Randall; courtesy of the MLTSR.)

Sand tufas are a special category of tufa formation. The mixing of calcium and carbonate occurred beneath the sandy bottom of the lake, and later, the sand castle–like structures were exposed as the lake dropped and loose surrounding sand blew away. They are found in scattered clusters along the south and east shores of the lake. (Photograph by Larry Ford; courtesy of the MLTSR.)

Three

THE KUZEDIKAS

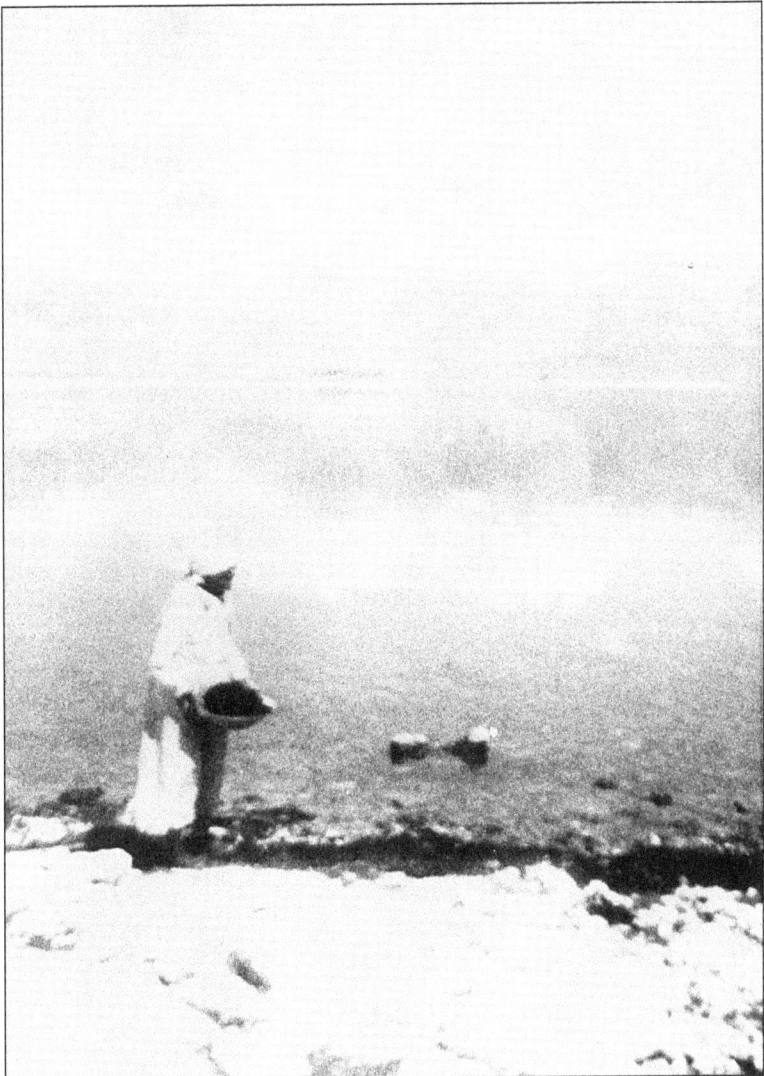

The Mono Lake Paiutes call themselves the Kuzedika. Here Nellie Charlie collects alkali fly pupae (*kutsavi*) on the south shore of Mono Lake near Rush Creek. The pupae are nutritious, providing fat and protein, and have a buttery taste. They were dried, stored, and traded with other people. The name "Mono" (pronounced with a long O sound) comes from the Yokuts, west of the mountains, and translates as "people of the flies." (Courtesy of the MLC.)

Mrs. Fitzgerald, a Mono Lake Paiute, is pictured with a basket full of caterpillars. In alternate years, the pandora moth (*Coloradia pandora*) caterpillars descend out of the Jeffrey pines in the forest south of Mono Lake. The caterpillars burrow into the ground to form cocoons to complete their life cycle. The Kuzedikas dug trenches around the trees to trap the caterpillars. They called them *piagi* and roasted or dried the caterpillars for later use, sometimes trading them with other Native American groups. The primary staple of the Kuzedikas' diet was piñon pine nuts. Rabbits, deer, and other animals were also hunted for food. (Courtesy of the MBHS.)

Mono Lake Paiute basket maker Tina Charley's work was often displayed in Yosemite National Park. Some of her incredibly fine baskets have, in recent years, sold at auctions for hundreds of thousands of dollars. (Courtesy of the MBHS.)

Nellie Charlie (left) and Carrie Bethel, Mono Lake Paiutes, carried these durable conical burden baskets, which were used for transporting items like pine nuts. Note the headband versus shoulder strap options on these two. Specialized baskets were also constructed for cooking and storage, and after tourists began coming to the region, ornamental baskets were made to appeal to outside buyers. (Courtesy of the MBHS.)

The Kuzedikas built temporary willow and brush homes as they moved up to the mountain meadows each summer to hunt and gather fresh greens, bulbs, and seeds. They survived challenging winters on the east side of the high-altitude lake basin in more substantial *tomaganis* built with juniper and piñon branches. Through the winter, they relied on stored piñon pine nuts and the skill of hunters. Warm rabbit-skin blankets were also valued trade items. (Courtesy of the USFS/INF.)

Kuzedikas play gambling games at Farrington ranch southwest of Mono Lake in this undated photograph. Such games were popular among Native Americans across the West. While one side sang and typically shook rattles, a small object was adroitly shifted from hand to hand. The object was to guess which hand held the hidden object when the singing stopped. (Courtesy of the MBHS.)

Four

THE SEARCH FOR GOLD

The greatest gold mining success in the region occurred just north of the Mono Basin at Bodie. At the 1881 peak in gold production, perhaps 10,000 people were in town that summer. Fewer stayed to endure Bodie's harsh winters at 8,400 feet. Much of the meat and produce that fed the town's populace came from Mono Lake ranches. (Courtesy of Bodie State Historic Park.)

Wood from forests ringing the Mono Lake Basin fueled steam-driven stamp mills, provided timbers to shore up Bodie's mining tunnels and shafts and lumber to build houses and business buildings, and made firewood to heat them. The wood had to come from miles away, and the forests rimming the Mono Basin were felled. Smaller loads of firewood were packed on mules, but for a time, steam ships carried major loads across Mono Lake, and wagons finished the trips through the Bodie Hills. (Courtesy of the USFS/INF.)

Above, logs are hauled to the Mono Mills southeast of Mono Lake in 1911 or 1912; note the size of the old-growth trunk sections. In 1881, thirty-two miles of railroad track were constructed around the east side of Mono Lake and north through the Bodie Hills to connect the Jeffrey pine forest south of the lake to Bodie. Though named the Bodie-to-Benton Railroad, it was never extended beyond Mono Mills. The *Mono*, the Bodie-to-Benton locomotive (below), hauls a load of cordwood in this undated photograph. In 1882, the railroad's first year of operation, it transported 5 million board feet of lumber and 27,000 cords of wood to Bodie. Firewood was the primary product hauled by the train as the years passed and less milled construction lumber was needed. (Both courtesy of the USFS/INF.)

Above, the mining community of Lundy celebrates Independence Day on July 4, 1900. Lundy Lake is visible in the distance. The Lakeview Dance Hall included a saloon and a dance floor built on car (or buggy) springs. The town was established in 1880 and served the May Lundy Mine and several other mines that made up the Homer Mining District. The peak population in Lundy Canyon coincided with the town of Bodie's greatest size, but it never exceeded 500 people. Below is the Jackson and Lakeview Mill at Crystal Lake, at the 9,000-foot elevation in Lake Canyon. That mill processed ore from the May Lundy, which was the most successful of the district's mines, producing $3 million worth of gold and silver. It was named for May, the daughter of W. J. Lundy, who had established a sawmill in the canyon in 1864. Today Lundy Canyon attracts fishermen and hikers with campgrounds, cabins, and access to the Hoover Wilderness. (Both, courtesy of Linda LaPierre.)

The Log Cabin Mine was located at 9,600 feet, high above Lee Vining with a panoramic view of Mono Lake. Jack Hammond recorded the first claim here in 1909. A year later, Jim Simpson filed on the same claim and named it the Simpson Mine. In 1930, the Mutual Gold Company bought the Simpson Mine. The Log Cabin Mine Company took over in 1939. Operations ended during World War II then resumed sporadically in later years. (Courtesy of the MBHS.)

This oil drilling derrick was on Paoha Island in 1908. In March that year, the Great Western Oil and Development Company drilled down to 2,500 feet, but no great pool of oil was ever found. Drilling core records helped establish the age of Mono Lake, as lake-bottom sediments extended below a volcanic layer deposited 760,000 years ago, indicating that the lake had been here continuously at least that long.

A car is parked outside the gate to the Leevining Ranger Station (note the spelling as one word) about 1923. The sign above the gate reads: "Leevining Ranger Station, District Ranger Headquarters; Information as to camping and fishing; Recreation maps obtainable." In 1908, Pres. Theodore Roosevelt established the Mono National Forest to manage timber, grazing, and recreational uses. The new national forest was formed from the portions of the original Inyo, Sierra, Stanislaus, and Tahoe Forest Reserves, which lay east of the Sierra Nevada crest. A 1930s Mono National Forest brochure cautioned recreational users that "It is better to carry a clear head on your shoulders than a big pack on your back." (Courtesy of the USFS/INF.)

Five

EARLY FARMS
AND RANCHES

This image shows Alice and Albert Sylvester about 1922. The Sylvester ranch was in the northwest corner of the Mono Basin and was one of the ranches and farms that served Bodie and the other mining towns with agricultural produce, such as potatoes, tomatoes, wheat, and corn, and livestock products. Albert worked the family homestead but was later also foreman of the Cain ranch south of Lee Vining, and the family lived there during those years. (Courtesy of RL.)

The Sylvester ranch was homesteaded by Albert's parents, Thomas and Emma Sylvester. The ranch included 50 acres of hay and pastureland, an apple orchard, and other cropland. The Sylvesters also owned additional cattle-grazing acreage in a meadow in Lee Vining Canyon, where they had better forage for the livestock. (Courtesy of RL.)

This was the Sylvester ranch house about 1922. Note the angled support on the left to keep the structure from leaning. Then as now, the Mono Basin winds occasionally challenged anything standing upright. (Courtesy of RL.)

From left to right, William, Hilda, and Margie, the children of Alice and Albert, pose in front of their house around 1918. There was also another daughter named Ruth in the family. Apple trees in the background had not leafed out yet that year. (Courtesy of RL.)

Albert Sylvester stands on the wheel cover of a tractor that features big, broad wheels for working in the soft sand typical of the Mono Basin. The two children are William and Margie Sylvester. The date is not known, but several years have passed since the 1918 photograph. (Courtesy of RL.)

The handwritten caption on the back of this photograph reads, "Alice and her flivver, about 1920." "Flivver" was the slang term for the Ford Model T; over 15 million of these assembly-line cars were sold between 1908 and 1927. (Courtesy of RL.)

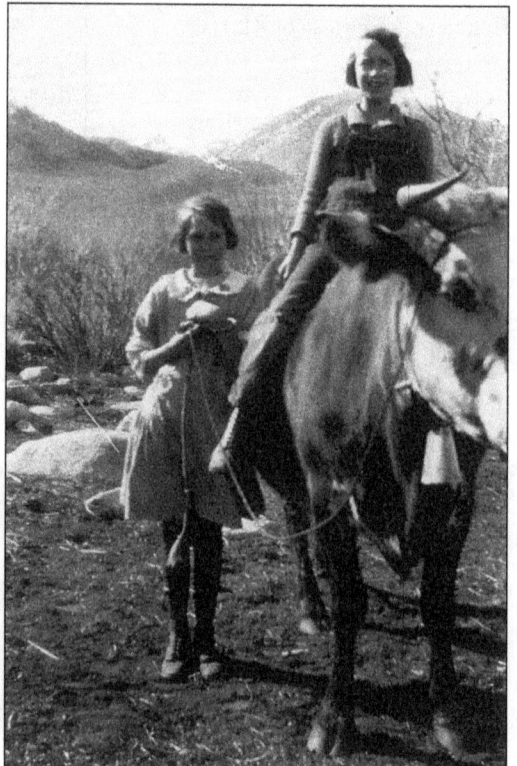

Pictured are Margie Sylvester (sitting on a cow) and a neighbor friend identified as Mary on the photograph (perhaps Mary Nay, whose family ranch was about 5 miles south of the Sylvesters'). According to the caption, the accommodating cow with the big bell was named Nellie. (Courtesy of RL.)

The Nay ranch and dairy was above the shore of Mono Lake and west of Lee Vining Creek. This photograph of Winslow Nay's family posing outside their house dates to about 1910. (Courtesy of RNE.)

A hollow tufa tower with a spring flowing inside of its cave served as a cool storage place for milk from the Nays' dairy. From left to right about 1910 are Louis McGowan and Lester Nay (standing on top of the rock) and Frank Shelton. The tufa tower this high above the shore of Mono Lake would have formed when ice-age Lake Russell covered this area. (Courtesy of RNE.)

The Nays' canopy-topped gasoline launch and a rowboat set out on Mono Lake on an unknown date. On May 31, 1898, Winslow Nay and five other men were in the Nays' launch when wind and waves capsized the boat about a mile from shore, and all six drowned. Only one body was ever recovered. This story is recounted in Margaret Calhoun's *Pioneers of Mono Basin*. (Courtesy of RNE.)

What remains of the Nay ranch pier is still visible today between the Scenic Area Visitor Center and the southwest shore of Mono Lake and not far from the cave tufa where milk was once stored.

NAY DAIRY HERD, MONO L. APPROX 1910

The caption written on this photograph states that this was the Nays' dairy herd about 1910, but they were probably on the Farrington ranch south of the current town of Lee Vining, since Bloody Canyon is visible in the background along the Sierra Nevada crest. Other ranchers moved their cattle within the basin to find grazing sites away from their primary homesteads. In 1899, a post office was established a half-mile north of the Farrington ranch at Crater for the ranch families that otherwise would have had to pay a toll to reach the post office at Mono Lake. (Courtesy of RNE.)

Potatoes, one of the Mono Lake Basin's most dependable root crops, grow on the Conway ranch in the northwest corner of the basin in 1922. The hill just to the north where Highway 395 climbs out of the basin is named Conway Summit. At 8,143 feet, it is the highest point between Mexico and Canada along that highway. John A. Conway moved down from Bodie after purchasing the ranch in 1903. (Courtesy of the MBHS.)

The Thompson ranch grows a crop of alfalfa in the summer of 1922. Some of the cottonwood trees and apple trees on this ranch are still visible to visitors to the Mono Lake County Park just above the northwest corner of the former lakeshore. The land is now owned by the City of Los Angeles, which leases a portion to Mono County for the park. (Courtesy of the MBHS.)

Jake Mattly's ranch, pictured in 1922, was southwest of Mono Lake. Note the large stack of hay behind the barn and the view of the Mono Craters in the background. Three families of Mattlys arrived in the Mono Basin at different times. John Mattly, Jake's cousin, had a ranch on the northwest shore of Mono Lake. Chris Mattly owned land where Lee Vining now stands and northward toward the lakeshore. (Courtesy of the MBHS.)

Potatoes were grown on the Chris Mattly ranch in August 1922. Potatoes do well in sandy soil and, as a root crop, are able to resist the Mono Lake Basin's tendency to produce hard freezes. The area's notoriously short growing season averages about 110 frost-free days a year. (Courtesy of the MBHS.)

A. Louis Camasco, the man on the right, harvests cauliflower and cabbage in September 1928 from his place on the southwest shore of Mono Lake (today the Dondero ranch). (Courtesy of the MBHS.)

By the 1920s, irrigated acreage in the basin had declined considerably from a peak of more than 4,000 acres in the 1880s. Above, A. Louis Camasco (left) shows off his zucchini crop in the late 1920s. He also grew carrots, potatoes, and rutabagas. (Courtesy of the MBHS.)

Rhubarb is harvested on the Goat Ranch in Mono Valley, north of Mono Lake, in August 1922. The ranch was established in 1889 by Joseph and Maria Scanavino, who converted a ranch that had raised goats into a vegetable produce farm, but the name "Goat Ranch" still persisted. Joseph died in 1908, and his son took over the ranch operation until the market for local produce ended. (Courtesy of the MBHS.)

Peas and beans were also grown on the Goat Ranch. The Scanavinos sold their produce in Bodie and Lundy, sometimes trading for cloth or staples like sugar and coffee. The farm was at a convenient location for travelers coming south out of Bodie at the base of the hills. One of the structures remaining there today was used as a schoolhouse after the Scanavino School District was established in the late 1890s to serve children from ranches in the north Mono Basin. (Courtesy of the MBHS.)

A second crop of alfalfa is coming up on the McPherson place in August 1922. Alfalfa was grown to feed livestock, and its ability to grow fast enough to yield two crops a year was particularly valuable. (Courtesy of the MBHS.)

In the 1920s, the McPherson family lived on Paoha Island, where they raised goats and had a kitchen garden that grew tomatoes, cabbage, beans, beets, onions, and lettuce. (Courtesy of the MBHS.)

The McPhersons had a spectacular winter view of the Sierra Nevada and Mono Lake from their ranch on Paoha Island about 1920. The residence is on the left, and barns and other outbuildings are also seen here. (Courtesy of the MBHS.)

In this closer view of the McPherson ranch house on Paoha, Helen Behymur stands with young Wallis McPherson in the kitchen garden. (Courtesy of the MBHS.)

Venita McPherson and her son (in the shade to the left of his mother) stand within an amazingly tall crop of corn grown on Paoha Island about 1920. (Courtesy of the MBHS.)

Captain Young is pictured on the left with Dorothy and George A. Robinson in 1931. Young's ranch was near the Mono Diggings site at the northwest corner of the Mono Basin. Captain Young was a veteran of World War I and was quite involved in local veterans events.

This is the house at the DeChambeau ranch as it appeared in 1931. The ranch was established north of Black Point in 1906. Louis DeChambeau had first moved down from Bodie onto property near the Sylvester ranch then relocated here to raise cattle, sheep, and chickens and grow alfalfa and vegetable crops. (Courtesy of Norman DeChambeau.)

The children pictured here around 1937 are, from left to right, Kent DeChambeau (10), Norman DeChambeau (8), and Phyllis DeChambeau (6). Today the DeChambeau ranch is within the National Forest Scenic Area, and its house and barn buildings have been stabilized. (Courtesy of Norman DeChambeau.)

Violet DeChambeau holds an armload of contented-looking sheep in May 1924 at DeChambeau ranch. She was born in Bodie and took many photographs with her box camera, but here she must have let someone else click the shutter. (Courtesy of Norman DeChambeau.)

A herd of sheep stirs up dust near the southwest shore of Mono Lake. The leader of this herd appears to be a goat wearing a bell. Large herds of sheep grazed in the Basin until the 1990s. Grazing allotments on federal land were mostly ended then to avoid transferring diseases fatal to the bighorn sheep population being reestablished on the mountain slopes west of Mono Lake. (Courtesy of the MLC.)

William Banta, pictured in 1994, kept an amazingly productive vegetable and flower garden going in Lee Vining all through his later life. As a young man, he began truck deliveries of produce from Bishop to the Mono Lake Basin before acquiring the Lee Vining Market in 1933.

Six

MONO LAKE RESORTS AND THE TOWN OF LEE VINING

The eastern base of the Sierra Nevada is a north-south travel corridor. Serving travelers has always been part of life in the Mono Basin. Here four cars in an Inyo Good Road Club Pasear tour group cross the Rush Creek highway bridge in the 1910s. The vehicle in the rear with the sign is a Studebaker.

A buggy is parked outside the Mono Lake Post Office at John Mattly's ranch (now the site of the Mono Inn) on the northwest shore of Mono Lake. Mattly was the first Mono Lake postmaster in 1889.

There was a tollgate operated by Andrew Thompson and Arch McNab to charge travelers on the highway along the west shore of Mono Lake. Pictured are, from left to right, Thompson, McNab, and an unidentified man. Brothers Jack and Dick Hammond took over operation of the place after Thompson died. Andrew Thompson was the first person to be buried in the Mono Lake Cemetery, on a hill overlooking the northwest shore of the lake.

Early luxury cars make a stop at Hammond's Store in 1905. The car in front is probably a Pierce-Arrow, though identification is uncertain, because in the first years of the 20th century, 2,200 makes of cars were manufactured in the United States. The Hammond brothers had earlier run a sawmill in Lundy Canyon and a different tollgate on Mill Creek.

William and Ruby Cunningham bought Hammond's Store in 1918 and renamed it the Tioga Lodge, gradually expanding the restaurant and lodging operations. Tioga Lodge was very close to the shore of Mono Lake in June 1942, when this photograph was taken. On the back of this Frashers Fotos postcard, someone wrote that lunch there had cost 85¢ and that they had been served by Japanese waiters—a special feature of the Tioga Lodge restaurant. (Courtesy of FFC.)

An early traveler by car heads north along the west shore of Mono Lake. At that time, the highway hugged the shore of the lake. Tall trees in the distance, above the point of land jutting into Mono Lake, mark the location of Tioga Lodge.

Note the unpaved highway and Mono Lake in this view from Conway Summit at the north end of the Mono Lake Basin. The Conway ranch is in the middle foreground, and a dark line of trees in the upper right marks the line of Mill Creek. (Courtesy of the Eastern California Museum, Mendenhall Collection.)

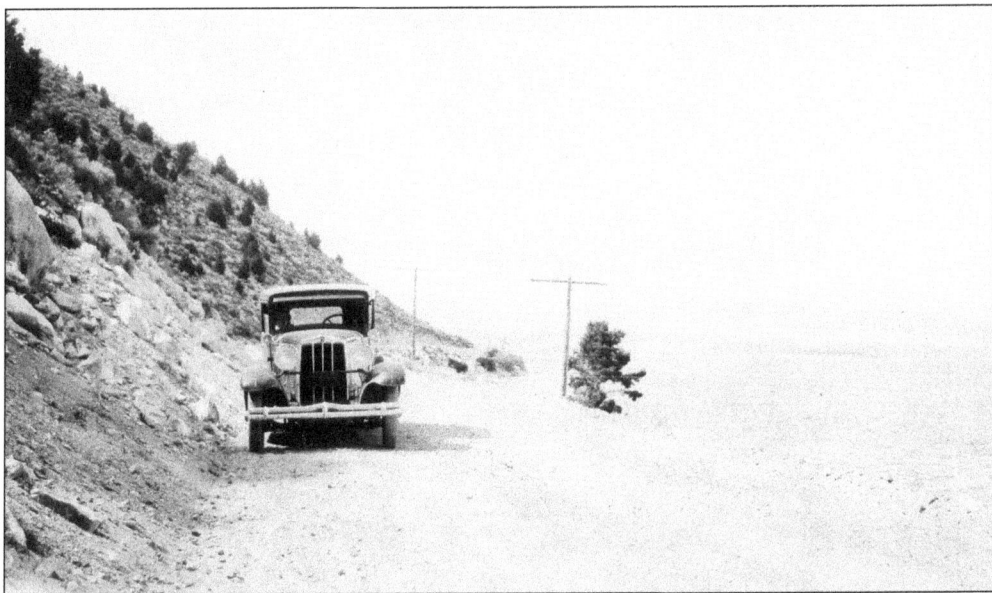

An unidentified traveler stopped to take this photograph sometime before 1932, the year the highway was paved. He was traveling south about halfway between the Tioga Lodge and Lee Vining.

The date of this photograph of Highway 395 south of Lee Vining is not known, but pavement is finally showing. The highway was given its federal designation as Highway 395 in 1926. It would not become four lanes along this stretch until the 1990s. The dark line of trees in the distance to the left of the road is cottonwoods on the Mattly ranch; stumps are all that can be found of them now. (Courtesy of the USFS/INF.)

The Frashers Fotos postcard label on the image above reads, "Lakeview Camp, Mono Lake, and Negit Island." The town of Lakeview was founded in 1926. Another community already had that name, however, so to satisfy the U.S. Postal Service, a new name, Leevining, was chosen, to honor Leroy Vining, the area's first settler. This photograph must have been taken before the name changed, so it was probably photographed around 1927. The spelling of the name Leevining as one word was still evident on business signs in the 1950s. At left is Chris Mattly, a native of Switzerland who acquired three parcels totaling 10 acres in 1926 near the junction of Highway 395 and the road over Tioga Pass to Yosemite. Mattly sold 10 lots for $50 each in the first year. (Above, courtesy of FFC; left, courtesy of MBHS.)

The El Mono Hotel was built in 1927 in Lee Vining by Peter Gilli (on the left). Also shown are Gilli's daughter, Rosemarie, and son, Peter Gilli Jr. Gilli bought two lots in the new town from Chris Mattly. He built the hotel in a "military style" he had learned as a Swiss army officer. The lobby was a restaurant, and the building housed a dentist office and a barbershop. (Courtesy of the MBHS; donated by George LaBraque.)

Today the El Mono Motel is one of the oldest buildings in Lee Vining. Its owners after Peter Gilli included Peter Conway, Morris Bewley and, for 30 years, Roger Kelly. Rooms can still be rented at the El Mono, and espresso coffee drinks and pastries are today served at the Latte Da Coffee Café in the motel lobby.

The Lee Vining Meat Market was built in 1925, and part of it is still standing. Bob Currie built the market to sell meat, bread, and produce. To the right is Burgan's Store and Restaurant, opened by Ed Burgan and his wife and turned over to their son-in-law, Glenn Mattly, in August 1925. At the far right edge of the photograph, Mono Lake can be seen in the distance; the lake was much higher than it is today.

This is a winter scene outside the market about 1932. Signs read "Leevining Home Bakery," "Cabins," and "Leevining Market." Additions were made to the original structure, which still exists as the office of the current market. Note the "Lakeview Camp" sign partially cut off on the left. The camp offered cabins and places for travelers to erect tents or park trailers. The motel on this site still serves travelers as the Lakeview Lodge. (Courtesy of RL.)

William Banta poses with his produce delivery truck before 1933. Note the bedroll hanging from the truck and the load of watermelons in the bed. He made deliveries of vegetables and fruit grown near Bishop in the Owens Valley, stopping along the June Lake Loop, in Leevining and Lundy, and all the way up to Bodie. With the collapse of mining in Bodie, many farms stopped producing in the Mono Lake Basin, so food grown 60 miles south in the Owens Valley became increasingly important for residents of the Mono Basin.

Another winter lineup of cars in 1937 shows the Lakeview Camp office and the Leevining market. Bob Currie sold the market and camp to William Banta in 1933. At one time, the business also provided a laundry room, bakery, and post office. (Courtesy of RL.)

About 1939, from left to right, owner William Banta and market employees Joe Merrill and Harry Blaver pose outside the Lee Vining Market. Blaver purchased the market from Banta in 1942, while the Banta family continues to own and operate the Lakeview Lodge.

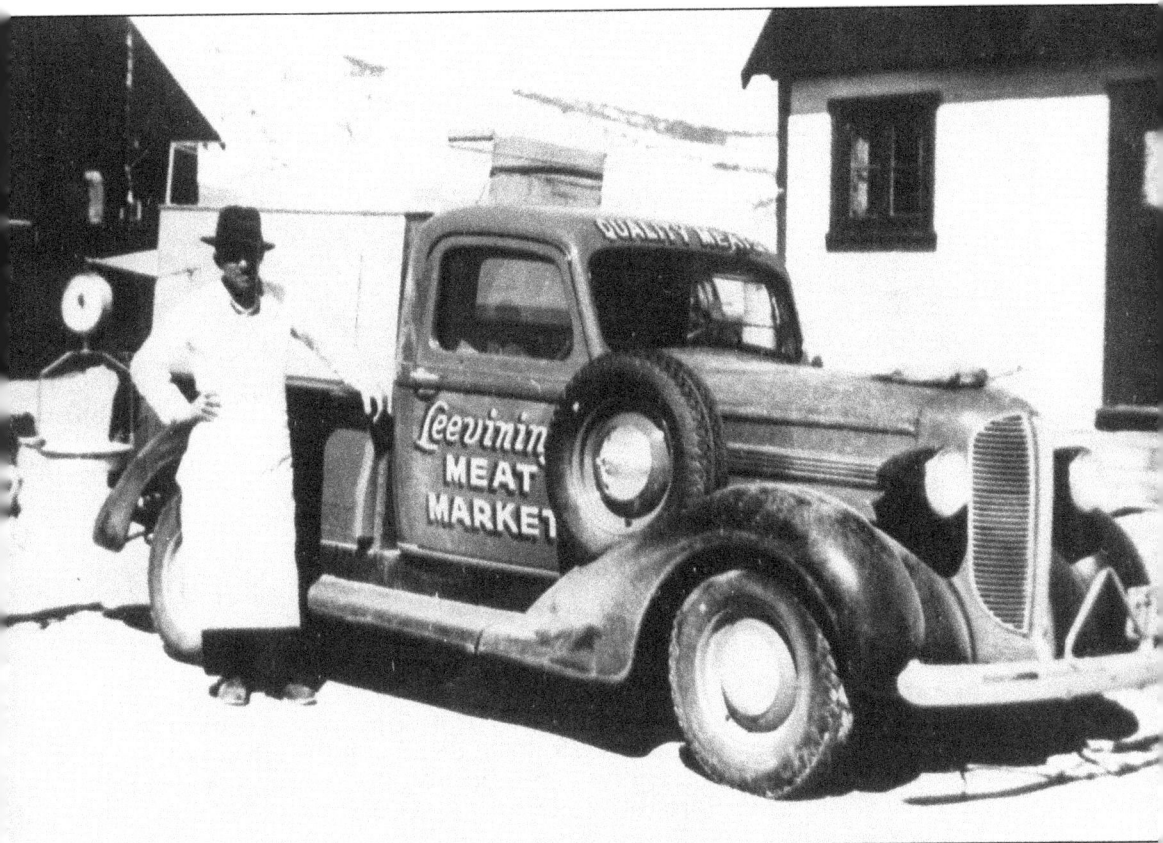

A dog appears to be very interested in the smells on the scales at the back of the Leevining Meat Market delivery truck about 1940. The driver shown here is Johnny Larson. Above the truck's windshield are the words "Quality Meats."

Julio's Sierra Café was established in 1940 in a building that was moved from Bodie to Leevining in 1928 by Henry and Margaret Calhoun. The Calhouns opened a bakery, market, and pool room and later sold to Julio Zunino. In 1965, this became Nicely's Restaurant, owned by Jim and Edna Nicely until 1995. To the right, part of a sign is visible for the Nevada Café, with a "coffee shop and fountain" sign.

The Nevada Café, bar, and restaurant was established by Mike Lazovitch, a Latvian, in the early 1930s. Though locals often referred to the place simply as "Bodie Mike's," the Nevada Café did not bear his name on its sign as it does today, under new ownership. (Courtesy of RL).

The Leevining Club, commonly referred to by locals as "Hess Hall," was in 1938 a dance hall and movie theater. The Hess family performed live music for dances that drew crowds of workers improving the Tioga Road, from the Log Cabin Mine, and from the Los Angeles aqueduct work camps. The business was established by Gus and William Hess in the early 1930s. Today it houses the chamber of commerce information center operated by the Mono Lake Committee. The original dance floor is still in place.

This overview photograph of Lee Vining was taken about 1941. Note the dark mass of trees—cottonwoods and pines—that marked where Lee Vining Creek ran down toward Mono Lake. The original route of the highway, seen in this image, leaves town toward Mono Lake following a route that would today take it past the town community center, east of the current highway alignment.

At the south end of Lee Vining in 1950, the Southern California Edison Power Plant is in the left foreground and the U.S. Pumice Plant on the far side of Lee Vining Creek. The pumice plant processes lightweight volcanic rock quarried at the south end of the Mono Craters. Much of the pumice is used for landscaping, but it is also made into toilet-cleaning and skin-abrading products.

The row of Lee Vining business buildings along the west side of the highway, as they appeared in 1953, includes the Leevining Market (left) and the Tioga Store ("Meats, Groceries, and Merchandise"). Across the street are the Sierra Café (now Nicely's Restaurant) and the Nevada Café (also known as Bodie Mike's).

The businesses along the east side of the highway in 1953 included the Richfield gas station, a sporting goods store, and Hess Garage. Businesses at the south end of town were on land leased from the forest service. It was not until 1967 that a land exchange was finalized in which 15 permittees in Lee Vining purchased 600 acres from other private parties and 30 acres from the City of Los Angeles to be added to the Inyo National Forest. In exchange, they received title to their properties in Lee Vining.

The Standard Oil plant on the west side of the road about 1946 later became a Chevron gas station. Gas stations, garages, motels, restaurants, and bars have served travelers as well as residents of Lee Vining ever since the town was established.

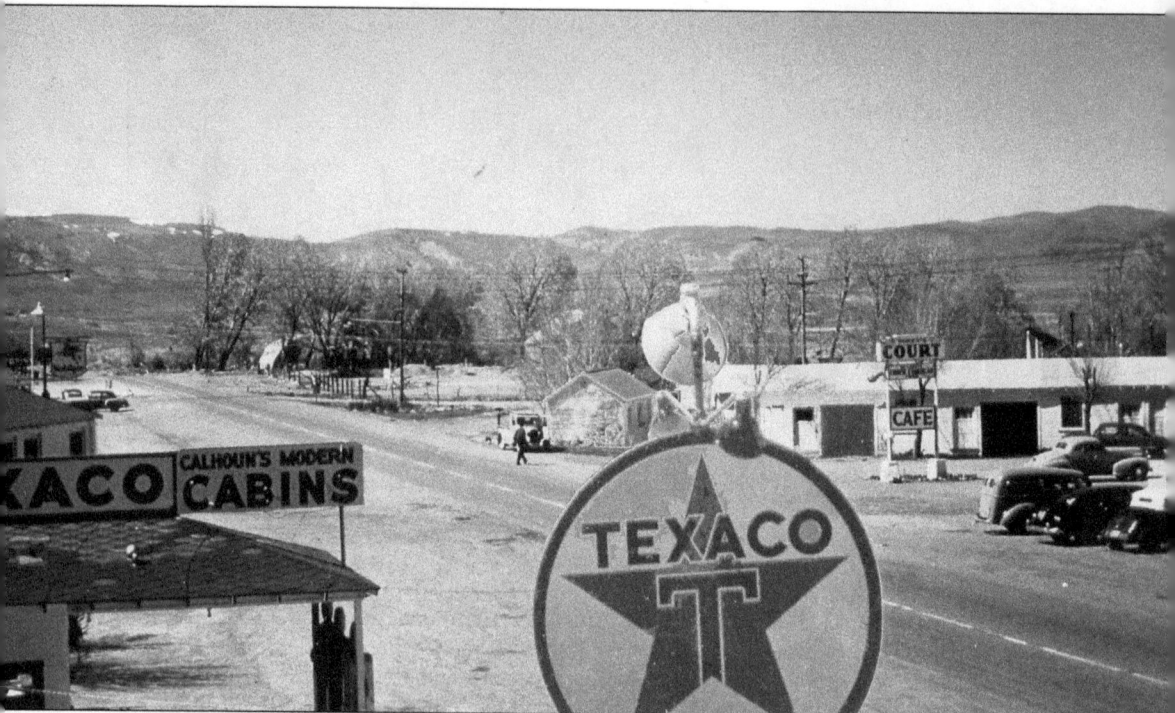

Texaco gas was pumped outside Calhoun's Modern Cabins. Note the small jail building across the highway, just behind the top-left portion of the round sign. The jail served the rowdy town in its roaring days in the 1930s and into the 1940s, but after World War II, the county no longer operated a jail in Lee Vining, and Don Banta was able to use that building as a community recreation room for the Boy Scout troop he led. The dark rectangles along the face of Honea's Court to the right of the jail were covered carports beside each room.

The Mono Inn, five miles north of Lee Vining, proclaimed itself "the place that made Mark Twain famous" after they inaugurated annual Mark Twain Days celebrations in 1928. Samuel Clemens visited Mono Lake in 1862 and wrote humorously about the area in *Roughing It*. This Frashers Fotos postcard was taken at the inaugural event as a bronze bust of Mark Twain was being dedicated. The bust did not stay outside the Mono Inn long; when the sculptor submitted a bill for $75 to proprietor Venita McPherson, she returned the bust to him, as she had understood it was being provided for free. From left to right are George Delury, Wallace McPherson (as Tom Sawyer), Betty Stewart (as Becky Thatcher), Dan Guis, Fred Walker, and Jim Stewart (as Huck Finn). (Courtesy of FFC.)

The first Mark Twain Days included beauty contestants representing Fales Hot Springs, the Mono Inn, Tom's Place, and the El Mono Hotel. Lily LaBraque, age five, won a silver dollar in this event. The festivities drew hundreds of people each year through the 1940s to speedboat and horse-swimming races, bathing beauty contests, baseball games, speeches, and other events. (Courtesy of FFC.)

Speedboat races were part of Mark Twain Days festivities at the Mono Inn. At least 65 people were in this 1933 shoreline crowd viewing the races. A chalkboard, right, appears to be the tally board for race results. The World Championship Hydroplane Races were held on Mono Lake in the 1930s. (Courtesy of Eastern California Museum, Ramsey Collection.)

Claude Walborn's hydroplane racing boat *Rowdy* was on Mono Lake during Mark Twain Days around 1938. Walborn accumulated a large trophy collection from his annual winning of the Mono Lake boat races. The alkaline lake water had to be thoroughly rinsed from boat motors after they operated in the lake to avoid a build-up of salt deposits.

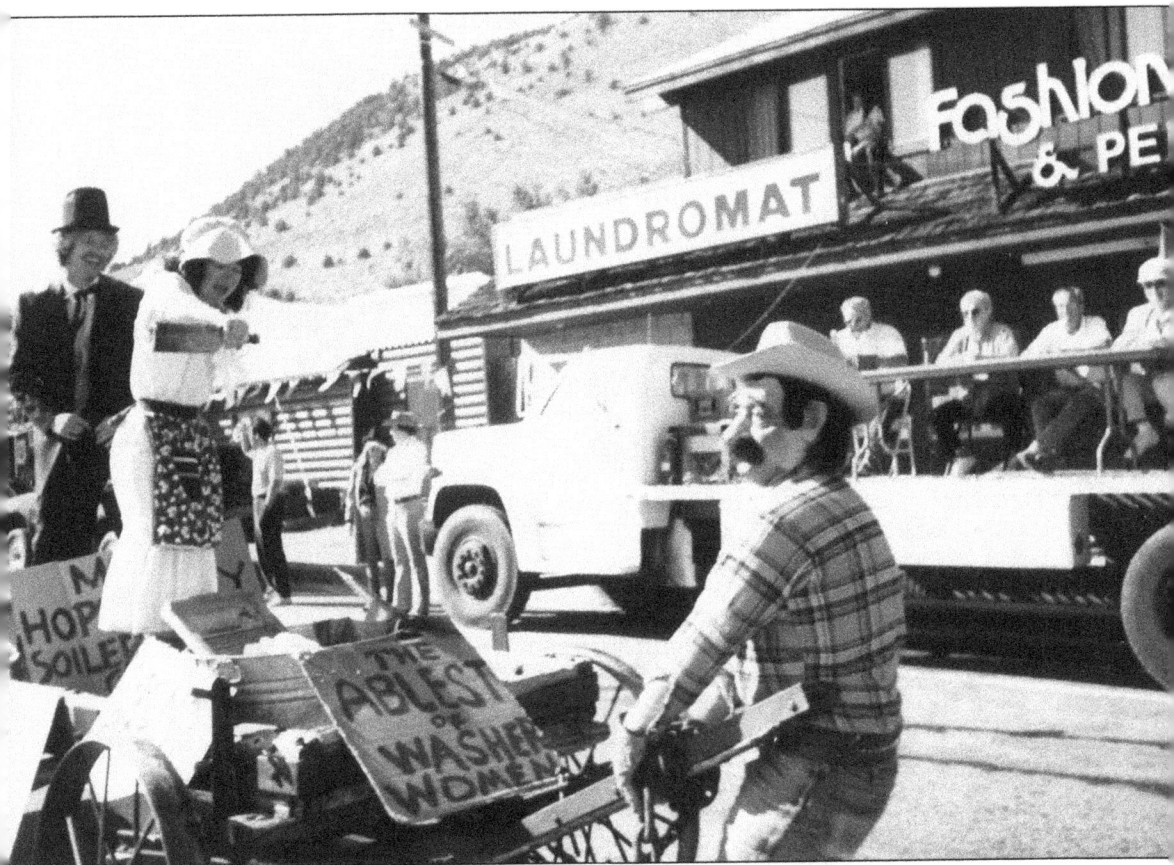

The Mark Twain Days festival has been revived several times, including in 1991, when a parade passed through Lee Vining. Ilene Mandelbaum was "The Ablest of Washer Women," a reference to a statement in Twain's book *Roughing It* that wetting clothes in Mono Lake's alkaline water made them "as clean as if they had been through the ablest washerwoman's hands." Floyd Griffin, wearing the mask, pulls the wagon. Richard Potashin, as the young Mark Twain (he was in his 20s when he came to Mono Lake), stands at the back of the float.

Through the 1930s, Wallis McPherson offered boat tours from the Mono Inn, at first on this excursion boat and later on the 36-passenger boat *Venita*, named for his mother. The summer boat tours included stops at the gull nesting colony on Negit Island. Today the nesting islands are closed to access to avoid disturbing the birds from April 1 through August 1 but can be reached by boat the rest of the year. (Courtesy of FFC.)

This is detail from a poster promoting the Mono Inn's boat tours: "This Week Visit Tahiti, The Tahiti of the Sierras, Paoha Island in Mono Lake." Tours began at the Mono Inn and occasionally were offered as moonlight excursions. The existence of hot springs on the south end of the island prompted the McPherson's goal of developing a "Tahitian" spa there, but the spa never opened.

The students at the Mono Lake School in 1896 (above) are, from left to right, (first row, sitting on porch) ? Filosena, Albert Sylvester, ? Filosena, Pearl Cavin, ? Filosena, Alice Sylvester, ? Nay, Herbert Dechambeau, and ? Currie; (second row) W. Currie, Emma Farneman (teacher), ? McGan, ? McGan, Isabel Nay, M. McKnight, A. Nay, J. Currie, M. McKnight, and Alice Currie. Bert Lundy is standing to the left. Orvis Nay is seated on a rock. This was the first Mono Lake School house, but not its first school. The Mono Lake School District was founded in November 1888. Until 1922, two schools existed in the Mono Basin. Crater School was south of Lee Vining near the Farrington ranch, located there so families would not have to pay the road toll at Hammond Station, and another was held for two years near Mill Creek in the ground floor of Jerry Miller's house. In 1889, this building was moved from Bodie to serve as a school at a site north of where the Mono Inn now stands. By 1922, the highway toll was no longer collected, and the school board had the building relocated closer to water northwest of Mono Lake. (Courtesy of the MBHS.)

In 1926, the Mono Lake kids attended school in a newer building constructed at the same location. Mildred Gregory taught the first term in the new school, which was used until 1942, serving grades one through seven. In 1987, the building was relocated to Hess Park in Lee Vining, and it now houses the Schoolhouse Museum operated by the MBHS. From left to right are (first row) Velma Rogers, Elma Hess, Betty Bergan, unidentified, Hilda Sylvester, and two unidentified; (second row) August Hess, William Sylvester, Danny Rogers, two unidentified, Mildred Gregory, Jack Bergen, Jean Bergen, Billy Nay, Margie Sylvester, Mary Nay, and Margaret Gilbert. (Courtesy of RL.)

Lee Vining High School girls in the 1941–1942 school year (above) include, from left to right, Patricia Hess, Roberta Adair, Bonnie Marks, Dorothy Harvey, Imogene Petty, and Josephine Hess. Teachers that year were Bertha Ypparaguerre and Kathleen Clover. Below is the high school building, which was located on the west of town; today the building is part of the elementary school. During World War II, the high school closed; some students boarded in Bishop and attended school there. (Both, courtesy of the MBHS.)

The Lee Vining school bus is parked in front of Hess Garage. Gus Hess stands beside the driver's door, and William, his brother, is to the left. This was the first local garage and gas station in Lee Vining. The year of this photograph is not known, but it was probably before 1930. Compare this image of Gus Hess to the photograph below. (Courtesy of the MBHS.)

In 1968, the Lee Vining/June Lake kindergarten class was taught by Merle Fronk. They were shown the volunteer fire department's truck by Gus Hess in October 1968. The children are, from left to right, (first row) Keri Murphy, Nicole Dondero, Paula Campbell, Terri Higgins, Margie Fronk, Lisa Dondero, and Stacy Auchiberry; (second row) Rick Murphy (in dark shadow by wheel), Rex May, David Bennett, Martin Perez, Ralph Keeler, Tony Pedro, David Montgomery (in the cab of the truck), and Bruce Parker.

The volunteer fire department had to deal with an arson fire that burned the Lee Vining High School on September 19, 1998. The 45 high school and junior high school students moved into temporary buildings while reconstruction occurred. Many of the fire department's response calls are to accidents along the nearby highways.

The Lee Vining town baseball team from 1948 through 1953 includes, from left to right, (first row) Richie Dondero, second base; Ray Washington, right field; Ted Williams, bat boy; Ernie Mike, center field; and Earl Hess, left field; (second row) John Dondero Jr., shortstop; Stan Hess, catcher; August Hess, pitcher and manager; Roy Dondero, third base; Mike Kelleher, first base; and Brick Wilcox, umpire and help coach. (Courtesy of the MBHS.)

The Lee Vining Reds Little League team played at the Walter Lantz baseball field in 2008. From left to right, the players are Juan Saldaño, Justin Hansen, and Juan Carlos Reyes. Walter Lantz, the famous Woody Woodpecker cartoonist, threw out the first pitch on the dedication day for the field. He owned a summer home at Silver Lake and also supported children's art in the June Lake and Lee Vining communities. (Photograph by Nicholas Carle.)

The Mono Marina was operated by Mono County on the west shore of Mono Lake in the 1950s and early 1960s. For a time, small sailboats could be rented there. The "Old Marina" site, just off Highway 395 a mile north of Lee Vining, is now one of the busier visitor sites in the Mono Lake Tufa State Reserve, with interpretive panels and a boardwalk to reach the lake across the shore-fringing wetlands. (Courtesy of the MLC.)

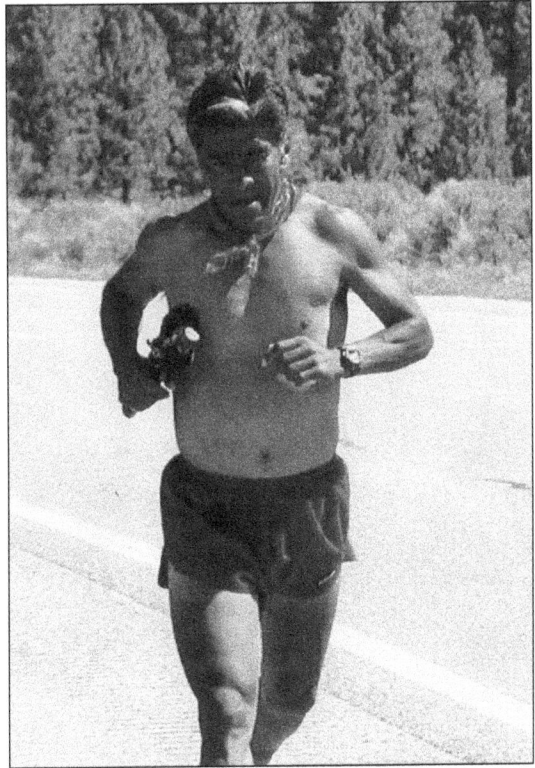

Greg Williams (at right), a local Kuzedika Mono Lake Paiute, is an excellent distance runner who participated in June 2002 when the 500 Mile American Indian Spiritual Marathon Relay passed through Lee Vining (below). The marathon relay is an annual event that begins in San Diego, passes through Lee Vining, and crosses over to the Bay Area.

The Lee Vining Community Presbyterian Church had been decorated by a snowstorm in February 1969. The church building was originally a school at the West Portal construction camp and was moved to town in 1941 after tunnel construction ended. (Courtesy of the MBHS.)

Our Savior of the Mountains Catholic Church in Lee Vining was also moved from West Portal, where it had been a dispensary building. The sacristy was used for living quarters before the rectory was added in the early 1950s. An artist friend of Fr. Christopher Kelley painted a picture that now hangs on the wall behind the altar of Christ superimposed on the scene of Tioga Pass and, with artistic license, Mono Lake in the distance.

Seven

THE JUNE LAKE LOOP

This Frashers Fotos Collection postcard scene is titled "Sierra Saddle Livery at Carson Camp on Silver Lake." Carson Camp was established in 1917, the first resort and pack station to operate on the June Lake Loop. Roy Carson was a carpenter for the Southern Sierras Power Company in 1916, when the Gem Lake Dam was built. The name was changed to Silver Lake Resort in 1940. The pack station is now operated as the Frontier Pack Station. (Courtesy of FFC.)

Carson Camp at Silver Lake was photographed on a day in 1922 when the lake was calm enough to act like a perfect mirror. The store and restaurant building at Silver Lake was constructed in 1921. Lumber for all of the cabins had to be hauled all the way from the Mammoth Saw Mill.

This is Culvers Camp at June Lake in August 1937. The first June Lake post office was established here in October 1927 with Harry Culver as postmaster. After 1932, Culver Camp was owned by the Gerths. (Courtesy of RL.)

Rodeos were regular events for the local cowboys. The 1949 location above is the Gull Lake meadows, still known as the rodeo grounds and now across from the June Mountain Ski Area. This photograph was taken by Leonard "Slim" Tatum, who owned the Silver Lake Pack Station. Below, they were bucking and roping way back in 1926 at a rodeo possibly held northeast of June Lake. (Above, courtesy of the MBHS; below, courtesy of RL.)

Movie actor Wallace Beery often flew his plane to June Lake; this photograph of Beery (the pilot) and Bud Kline (standing) was taken in 1932. The Hollywood crowd, including wealthy residents of Pasadena, started visiting before 1920 and established a row of cabins behind Silver Lake, sometimes called "Little Pasadena" or "Millionaires Row," Clark Gable, Greta Garbo, and director Frank Capra were some of the more famous visitors. As early as 1918, there was an airstrip near June Lake. (Courtesy of FFC.)

Beery had a house on a small island at the southwest end of Silver Lake. On February 2, 1937, an avalanche slid across the frozen lake and demolished Beery's unoccupied cabin and six other cabins nearby. (Courtesy of RL.)

Marshall's Landing on June Lake has its rental boats lined up and ready to go in this Frashers Fotos postcard. The June Lake Marina, Boulder Lodge (the second resort on the loop), and other resorts today satisfy the fisherman's need for boats, bait, refreshments, and lodging. (Courtesy of FFC.)

RUSH CREEK TROUT EGG TAKING STATION

The Rush Creek egg-taking station was also photographed by Burton Frasher of Frashers Fotos. The fish traps were on Rush Creek between Silver Lake and Grant Lake. The first Fish and Game Department hatchery on the June Lake Loop was set up in tents at Silver Lake. In 1926, the Fish and Game Department established the Fern Creek fish hatchery upstream from Silver Lake and spread the recreational activity into what had previously been fishless Eastern Sierra waters. Fishing became a major local attraction, and the lakes and streams of the June Lake Loop became fabled for their cutthroat and brown trout. (Courtesy of FFC.)

Another Frashers Fotos postcard taken at Carson Camp shows limit catches of trout. There are at least six dozen fish on those strings held by six men! The sign on the building reads "Carson Camp, where fly fishing is always good. Boats, Grocery, Cabins, Tents." (Courtesy of FFC.)

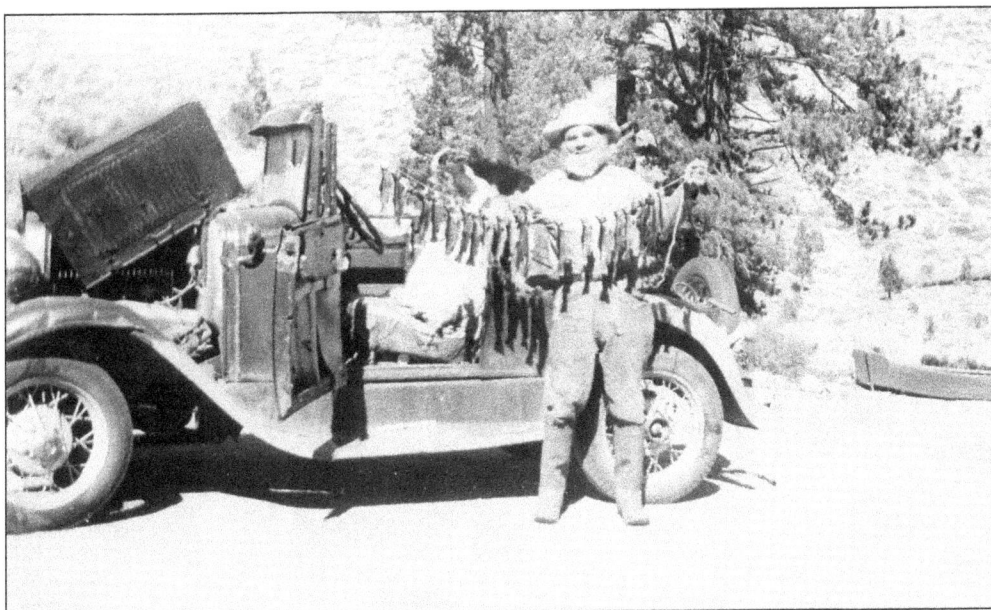

Roy Davis, also known as "Frenchie," caught this impressive string of trout at Little Walker Lake about 1950. Davis was a colorful character who worked as a handyman, sign painter, and fishing guide from the Tioga Pass area to the June Lake Loop.

Fish catches were big in both numbers and size of fish back in the day. In 1940, Slim Everett (left) and George Heinselman are shown with four exceptional trout from June Lake. Everett was a local character on the June Lake Loop who earned the name "Stew Pot" by daily washing his work clothes using an old stew pot as a washtub. He moved to Alaska to seek a more secluded lifestyle after hearing that a ski resort was to be developed in the June Lake area. A small food shack at the base of Chair Seven on June Mountain today bears his name.

In 1940, Alfred (left) and William Banta came home with this string of fish from Grant Lake (above). The next year, in 1941, William Banta pulled these three big ones (left) from June Lake. Both photographs were taken at the Banta residence next to Lakeview Lodge in Lee Vining.

Walt Dombrowski (right) was photographed with a visitor at his Mono Lake hunting club near the mouth of Rush Creek. Thousands of waterfowl, including shovelers, mallards, and geese, came to the stream delta and to four man-made ponds Dombrowski dredged on either side of the creek. The ponds were at different elevations, and water from Rush Creek spilled from one to another. Waterfowl numbers declined as Mono Lake dropped after 1941 but are improving again today. (Courtesy of the MLC.)

Carrie Webb poses with furs from animals trapped by Al Gardisky near his Tioga Camp in 1925. Gardisky's place would eventually become the Tioga Pass Resort. Carrie was married to Al Webb, who worked for the Southern Sierras Power Company.

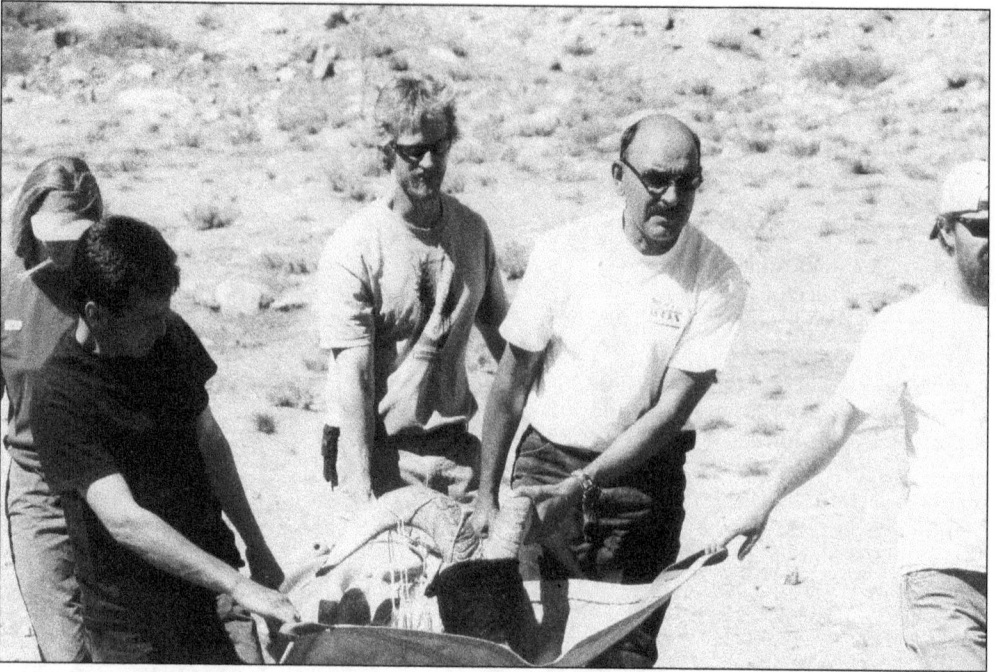

The native bighorn sheep had disappeared from the mountains above Lee Vining until a herd was reestablished in Tioga Canyon with transplants from the southern Sierra Nevada in 1986. Above, a blindfolded ram is carried from the helicopter to the release point along Highway 120. The man holding on to the sheep's horn is veterinarian Dr. Ben Gonzales. Though the sheep are generally shy, travelers along Highway 120 now and then are treated to a sight like this below. A ram drinks from the small water channel just a few feet from passing cars in May 2008.

Eight

WINTER CHALLENGES AND RECREATION

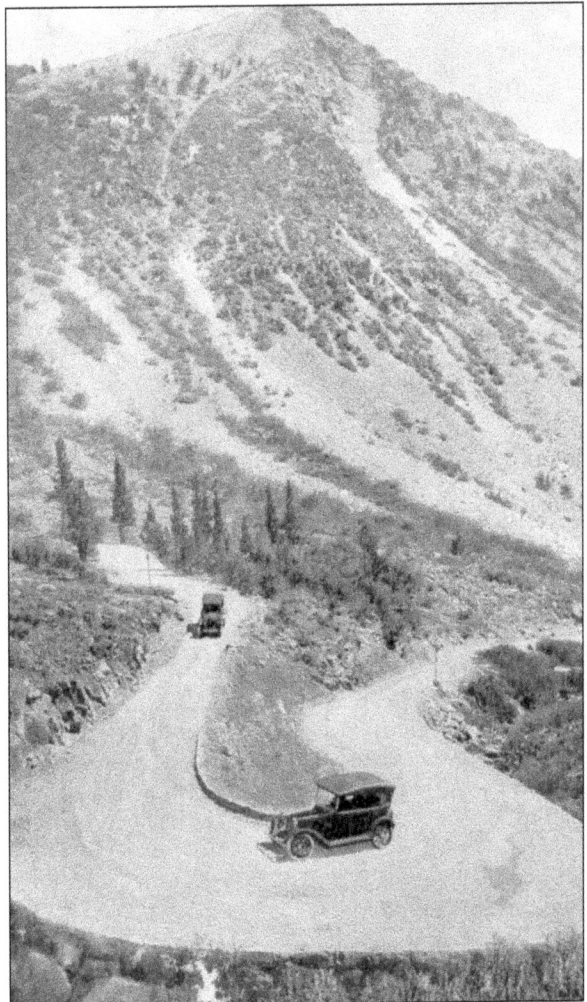

In this 1922 postcard, cars negotiate the tight turns near the Warren Fork of Lee Vining Creek. In 1915, the National Park Service dedicated the Tioga Pass Road, originally a rugged wagon road. That year, 350 cars made the unpaved crossing between Lee Vining and Yosemite Valley. It was not until 1937 that the Tioga Pass Road was paved all the way across. This card was mailed in June 1922 with the message that there had been 30 feet of snow on the curve shown on the postcard earlier that winter. (Courtesy of the MBHS.)

The opening of the pass was celebrated each year in the 1920s with a community fish fry sponsored by Lee Vining business owners. The late-spring opening and early-winter closures of Highway 120 across Tioga Pass have always controlled the annual influx of tourists and travelers to Lee Vining. (Courtesy of the Yosemite National Park Library.)

Tioga Pass is the highest highway pass in California at 9,945 feet above sea level. As in 1926, when the photograph above was taken, it remains a popular place to stop and take a photograph at the Yosemite National Park eastern gate. Below, the park gate is still marked by stone pillars, but an entrance station to collect fees has been added. This photograph was taken on December 20, 1998, when the road was closed to vehicles for the winter. Note the snow on the highway; by late winter, it would be completely buried. (Above, courtesy of RL.)

The Tioga Camp in 1922 was no longer named Gardisky's Camp. Later its name would change again to the Tioga Pass Resort. In this view, the direction of travel is from the national park gate towards the resort; the unpaved highway continued down toward Lee Vining Canyon. Lee Vining Creek runs beside the road. (Courtesy of the MBHS.)

Joseph Scanavino's car is stuck in the snow in 1920. Note the chains on the tires. As early car engines became weaker from use, it was common to cut down the car, taking off unnecessary body parts to lighten the load. Living above 6,000 feet in the Eastern Sierra, with nearby slopes that are over 13,000 feet above sea level, brought challenging winter weather.

On Highway 395, a mile south of Crestview (above), from left to right, Don Banta, Ellen Banta, and Cliff Banta stop in 1939 to measure the height of the snowbank cut by plows. It seems irresistible, in such big winters, to take photographs like these with one's car posed against the snowbank. Comparing the snow depths and the models of cars makes for an interesting historical record. Below is the 1954–1955 winter, and the boy standing on the bumper of the Pontiac is Glen Lewis. (Courtesy of RL.)

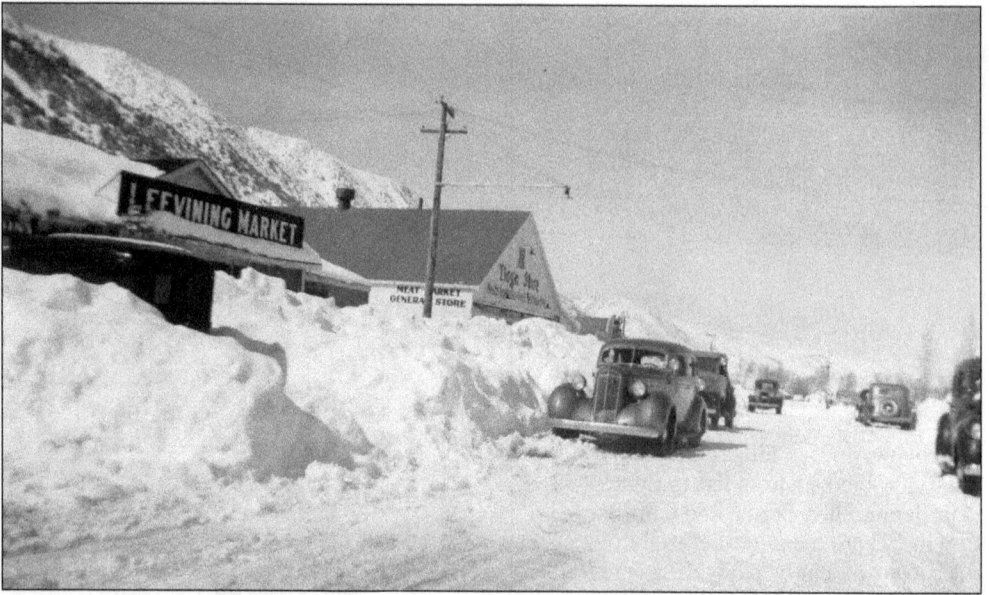

Heavy snow in towns is always a challenge. Roads have to be plowed before traffic can move again. This was how the main street of Leevining looked after a blizzard in 1938.

The "Happy Motoring" sign seems ironic as travelers dig out after a night of heavy snowfall in Lee Vining in the exceptionally big winter of 1969. This photograph was mailed to the Lakeview Lodge by one in a group of 10 young men who got stuck in town during the blizzard. They ran out of money and were grateful that they were allowed to stay their last night for free. (Photograph by Mick Caughey.)

Tex Cushion's dogsled mushed to Leevining in 1935. When major snowstorms closed roads, Tex would deliver the mail to communities between Mammoth Lakes and Leevining. Local residents George and Steve Allison were mushers. This picture was taken in front of Bodie Mike's and shows George LaBraque standing and Lily and Georgie LaBraque sitting in the sled.

In the winter of 1929, Leevining boys (left to right) Howard McAffee, Cliff Donnelley, Jim Keller, Stan Hess, and Larry Hess decided to make the biggest snowball ever on the Leevining school grounds.

Carrie Webb (left) and Alice Sylvester are shown here single-pole skiing. Skis were manufactured locally for sale by Louis DeChambeau of Lee Vining. He made 9-foot-long men's skis and 7-foot skis for women. The skis were strapped to regular boots. One wooden pole was dragged (or sometimes held between the legs and sat on) to control speed and aid turns. (Courtesy of RL.)

Walt Dombrowski, owner of a Rush Creek ranch, skis toward a rope tow ski lift. Though he is credited with building the first rope tow on the hill above Leevining, this is another, unknown location. In 1938 and 1939, other rope tows were operated by ski clubs. (Courtesy of VBR.)

Walt Dombrowski is on skis, and Ellen Dombrowski Miller is the passenger on the dogsled. Rope tows were free to skiers in those years within the Mono Basin on the slopes of Conway Summit, near Oh! Ridge (the approach to June Lake from Highway 395), on the Aeolian Buttes above West Portal, and at other locations. (Courtesy of VBR.)

Locals often skied on the steep hills behind Leevining. From left to right, these boys are Alan Blaver, Harry Blaver Jr., and Gus White around 1948 to 1950. (Courtesy of RL.)

The Lee Vining High School ski team in 1953 were champions of the Sierra Nevada Interscholastic Ski Federation. The large skis were used for ski jumping. From left to right are Don Hess, Ron Donnelley, Jim Blessing, Harry Blaver Jr., Frank Cassidy, Gus White, and Dick Miller. Coach Don Banta holds the championship trophy.

The rope tow ski lift behind Leevining, seen here in 1959, served the Mono Ski Club and Leevining High School competitive ski teams. The school ski team was coached by Don Banta. They traveled as far as the San Bernardino Mountains of Southern California and up to Lake Tahoe to compete.

The skiers on a sunny winter day in Lee Vining in 1956 are, from left to right, Nick Cassidy, unidentified, Jack Murphy, Sharon Murphy, Don Banta, Skipper Hess, Glen Lewis, Blake Brinkenopff, two unidentified, and Jim Blessing.

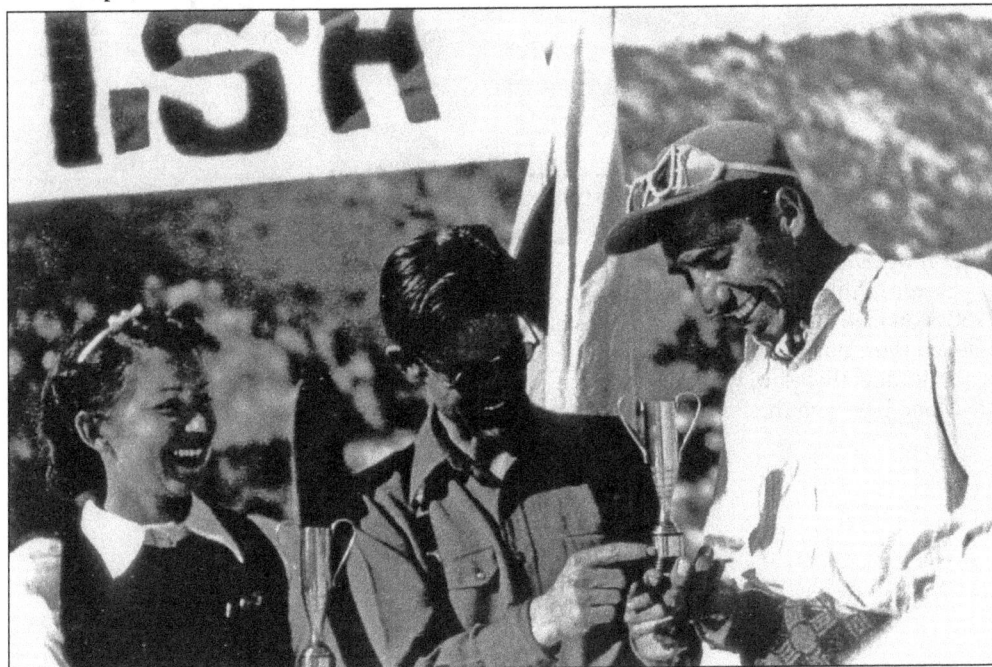

Slim Mayberry (middle) admires the trophy won by Eunice Yongue (left) and August Hess in the double-slalom ski race at Osborne's June Lake ski lift around 1940. This was probably the first double-slalom race ever run. In this event, the times for teammates are combined. This location was down canyon from the present June Mountain Ski Area.

After nine months of construction, June Mountain Ski Area opened in February 1961 under a use-permit William C. "Bud" and Lois Hayward secured from the Inyo National Forest. Here, in 1960, workmen perch at the top of the face, where the breakover towers at the top of Chair One reached the Chalet Lodge. Views from the June Mountain Ski Area are spectacular. Gull Lake is almost directly below, with June Lake in the distance beyond the towers. Far in the distance are Mono Lake and the Bodie Hills. (Courtesy of WH.)

Above, the aerial view of June Mountain in 1960 shows how thickly forested it was before ski runs were created on the slopes. Mammoth Mountain is labeled in the distance, and a proposed route for the first lift to the top of June Mountain is drawn onto this image. Gull Lake is in the foreground, a white expanse of snow on ice. Below is a view from a similar angle taken in the mid-1970s, after ski runs had been created. The ski area became a major part of the winter economy in northern Mono County, employing about 150 people during each ski season. The image below also shows the three zones of the June Mountain Ski Area that shaped use patterns on the mountain: a very steep lower face, a middle zone offering opportunities for several easier runs, and the top of the mountain with challenging black-diamond routes for expert skiers. (Courtesy of WH.)

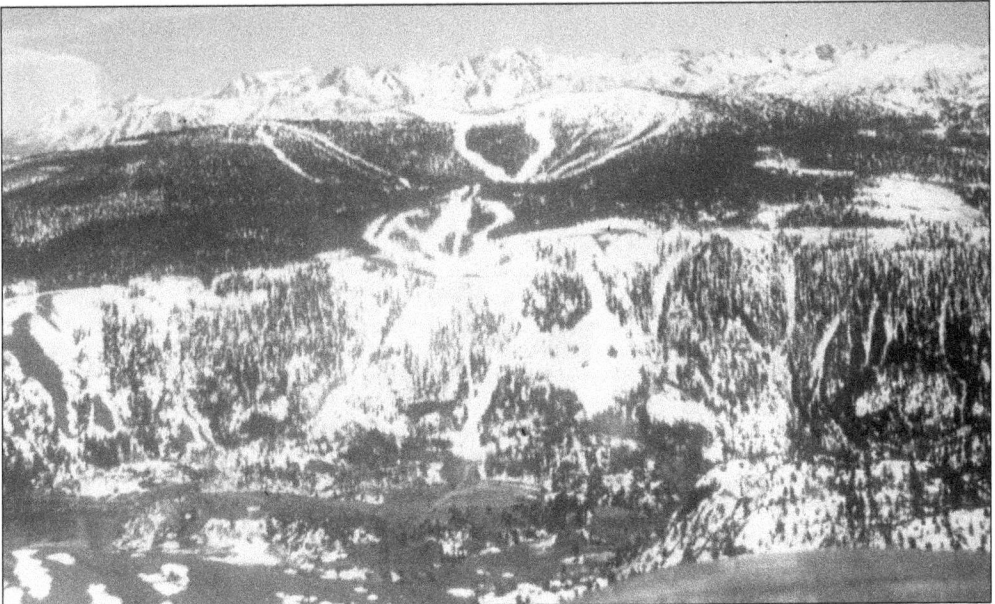

As this photograph taken about 1963 shows, only Chair One, a T-bar frame, and a Poma Lift operated at first from the Chalet bowl, where a thick forest had been cleared to establish the runs. Chair Two was added in the mid-1960s, and skiing opportunities kept expanding. Construction never really stopped despite economic challenges for a ski resort in the relatively small community. (Courtesy of WH.)

William C. "Bud" and Lois Hayward, who owned and developed the June Mountain Ski Area for 26 years, pose on the top of June Mountain about 1963. Reverse Peak is at the far right in the middle distance, dwarfed by the Sierra Nevada crest in the background. Part of the horseshoe-shaped canyon that wraps around Reverse Peak is just beyond the darkly forested plateau. Since 1986, the June Mountain Ski Area has been owned by Mammoth Mountain. (Courtesy of WH.)

Nine

A SOURCE FOR WATER AND POWER

In 1910, a power plant is under construction by the Pacific Power Corporation near the old mining town of Jordan, using water diverted from Mill Creek in Lundy Canyon. A dam was built to raise Lundy Lake, a few miles to the south, for water storage to serve the Jordan hydroelectric plant. (Courtesy of the Mono County Historical Society.)

On March 11, 1911, an avalanche demolished the Jordan power plant and buried homes, killing seven people. Rescuers from the Mono Lake area were supplemented by men who skied from Bodie, 20 miles away. After 64 hours, one woman, Agnes Mason, and her dog were found alive. A new Mill Creek powerhouse was completed in December that year closer to Lundy Canyon. It still provides power to Southern California Edison customers. (Courtesy of the Mono County Historical Society.)

The Rush Creek hydroelectric powerhouse was completed in December 1917 by the Pacific Power Corporation. Ownership shifted in 1917 to the Nevada-California Power Company, then in 1922 to a subsidiary of that company named the Southern Sierras Power Company, then to the California Electric Power Company in 1941, which merged with Southern California Edison in 1964. Rush Creek water is stored behind dams forming Waugh, Gem, and Agnew Reservoirs and drops 1,810 feet to turbines at the powerhouse near Silver Lake.

A pack needs adjustment on the trail to Agnew Lake in 1922 as material is being hauled up the steep trail for the Agnew dam. Ernest Bulpitt and Francis Banta are probably two of the men in the photograph. (Courtesy of VBR.)

To facilitate movement of workers and material up the steep 1,250-foot climb above the Rush Creek powerhouse to Agnew Lake (at 8,506 feet), a tramway was constructed. In 1938, several unidentified people take the ride on the tramway, which was 4,800 feet long. Rails and cars for the trams came from a mine in Bodie that was no longer operating. (Courtesy of VBR.)

A second section of tramway was built from Agnew Lake up to the Gem Lake Reservoir at 9,065 feet. Construction materials were brought up on the lower tram and then floated on barges across Agnew Lake. This tramway section was 1,600 feet long. The dam to form the Gem Reservoir covered up three small natural lakes. Agnew was originally one smaller lake. (Courtesy of the MBHS.)

The Poole Plant hydroelectric station at the bottom of Lee Vining Canyon receives water descending almost vertically for 1,600 feet. Water first travels through a tunnel from Ellery Lake (earlier known as Rhinedollar Lake) at the 9,500-foot elevation. The upstream facilities in this system also include Tioga Lake (at 9,650 feet) and the Saddlebag Reservoir (at 10,050 feet). (Courtesy of USFS/INF.)

The Southern Sierras Power Company completed the Lee Vining No. 1 Power Plant in 1924 as part of its Lee Vining Creek hydroelectric power system. The plant was renamed in honor of Charles Oscar Poole in 1925, after the chief engineer's death. Today the hydroelectric system is owned by Southern California Edison. Besides the powerhouse along the upper reaches of Lee Vining Creek, there is a substation in the town of Lee Vining. (Courtesy of the MBHS; photograph by Glenna Clark.)

A Caterpillar is seen pulling a sled with steel pipe, drums, and other material to build the Lee Vining No. 1 Power Plant at the head of Lee Vining Canyon about 1923. The Southern Sierras Power Company built a road from the Southern Pacific Railroad station in Benton, coming south of Mono Lake, to reach the base of Lee Vining Canyon.

Clarence Rhudy participated in a Bishop-to-Lundy survey trip around 1915 to 1920. As an engineer for the Nevada-California Power Company, Rhudy would help build the power plant in Lee Vining in 1923 and worked on the Poole Plant and Rhinedollar (Ellery Lake) facilities from 1923 to 1930. (Courtesy of VBR.)

Children Vance and Florence Rhudy stand outside Headquarters Camp Cabin No. 4, near the Poole Plant. Note the 1926 Dodge Brothers roadster. The initial development by the power company was difficult because of the remote and mountainous location. The company had a hard time hiring and keeping men on the job, so it went to considerable trouble to make living and working conditions as pleasant as possible. The note with this photograph says that the fence was added to this home "for the Rhudy children" and that Cabin No. 4 was "one of eight cabins." (Courtesy of VBR.)

The Lee Vining Creek Intake No. 3 was built in 1923 to send water down to the Lee Vining No. 3 Power Plant, which was located near the junction of Highway 395 and Highway 120. Operated by the Southern Sierras Power Company at first, it is now a Southern California Edison facility. Note the Dodge Brothers roadster parked off to the distant right and a half-dozen men working above the bridge. (Courtesy of VBR.)

This is a later view of the Intake No. 3 site along Lee Vining Creek after the diversion dam was completed. Large chunks of ice had backed up behind the dam. After 1933, the power plant this diversion had served in Lee Vining would be converted to a power company substation. (Courtesy of VBR.)

Ten

SAVING MONO LAKE

The West Portal construction camp was the largest of four camps for workers building an 11-mile tunnel beneath the Mono Craters. The tunnel entrance was covered to keep snow off rails that carried carloads of workmen to the tunnel face and hauled excavated material out to dump piles. Work began in 1934 on the Los Angeles Department of Water and Power's extension of its aqueduct in the Owens Valley to take streams flowing to Mono Lake. Diversions facilities and conduits would be built at Lee Vining Creek, Walker Creek, and Parker Creek, and a dam was constructed to enlarge the existing Grant Lake Reservoir on Rush Creek. Grant Reservoir stored water from all four creeks and controlled flows into the new tunnel. (Courtesy of FFC.)

The building at the far left is the West Portal hospital, a modern facility in the late 1930s that was staffed by two doctors and nurses and included an operating room and X-ray laboratory. The hospital also served the medical needs of June Lake and Leevining during the construction years. The next several structures in the photograph are dormitories for workers, housing two to a room. The larger building just right of center is the mess hall and commissary store. Offices and equipment buildings are on the far right. In the distant left are two rows of residences for supervisors. The vertical lines on the hill behind the residences mark the West Portal rope tow ski area. (Courtesy of Harry Weller.)

A group of workmen gathers outside the West Portal tunnel entrance in 1940. As many as 1,500 workers labored at the project, working seven days a week in three shifts that ran 24 hours a day during the six years of construction. They were challenged by lethal carbon dioxide gases under the volcanic craters and flooding water. The tunnel would not only carry stream water but also act like a horizontal well, tapping groundwater along its route. Those construction years were like a wild-west boom era for Lee Vining and June Lake, with saloons and dance halls doing a lively business. (Courtesy of Woody Carrington.)

West Portal workmen pose in 1940, the year the tunnel was completed. Workers in West Portal and East Portal construction camps began tunneling from each end, while at camps called Shaft One and Shaft Two, other workers descended elevators that intersected the 11-mile tunnel route. From the vertical shafts, tunneling could go in two directions, so a total of six headings were worked simultaneously. Water emerging at East Portal was added to the flow of the upper Owens River heading toward a new dam being built in the Long Valley. After Crowley Reservoir was complete, the Mono Basin facilities were dedicated in 1941. (Courtesy of Woody Carrington.)

Many of the workmen brought families with them to the Mono Basin, so the City of Los Angeles constructed a West Portal schoolhouse, and Mono County supplied a teacher. As scaffolding is visible, the school was apparently just being finished when this photograph was taken, probably in 1935. This building would be moved after West Portal construction activity ended to Lee Vining to serve as the Community Presbyterian Church.

112

Some unusual things happened at Mono Lake in the years before its water issues took center stage. In the 1950s and 1960s, the Army Corps of Engineers and the navy conducted explosion tests in Mono Lake (right) to study how bombs can generate large waves. With no fish in the lake, the impacts on lake resources were considered minimal at the time. In 1983 (below), two years after the Mono Lake Tufa State Reserve was established, volunteers from the Sierra Club gathered several miles of detonating wire that had lain on the bottom of the lake and been exposed as the lake dropped. The wire was recycled for its copper. The area has been called Navy Beach ever since the 1960s. (Both, courtesy of the MLTSR.)

The striking scenery of the Mono Lake Basin has featured in a number of Hollywood movies and television commercials. Above, *Fair Wind to Java* was a 1953 pirate film featuring the eruption of the Krakatoa volcano. One of the islets in Mono Lake served as the base of the volcano, and portions of the set that was constructed there remain in place. Today (below), the Krakatoa movie set serves as temporary shelter for researchers who study the gull-breeding population each summer. Another notable film made at the lake was Clint Eastwood's *High Plains Drifter*, filmed in 1973 on a point west of the South Tufa area. (Below, photograph by Janet Carle.)

In 1978, the former Hess Hall building became the Mono Lake Committee Information Center. Four of the streams that fed Mono Lake had been diverted since 1941 to supply water to Los Angeles. As a result, the lake fell 45 feet by 1982. The impacts of diversions on Mono Lake gradually became apparent. With half as much water, the salinity of the alkaline lake doubled. Life in the lake was threatened by the increasingly harsh water. In 1978, the Mono Lake Committee, along with the National Audubon Society, sued Los Angeles. Later CalTrout joined the effort, because fish and game law prohibited the complete dewatering of creeks by the city's water diversions. (Courtesy of the MLC.)

As Mono Lake declined, tufa towers began to emerge. On the north shore, these two towers with distinctive shapes served as benchmarks showing the lake's decline between 1962 (above) and 1978 (below). Mono Lake hit its lowest historic point in 1982 at 6,372 feet above sea level, 45 feet below its elevation in 1941, the year stream diversions began. At the lowest point, the lake held half as much water, and its salinity had doubled, approaching thresholds for life in the lake. Air quality became another issue as thousands of acres of salt flats were exposed. Wind produced increasingly severe dust storms that were dangerous to human health and violated federal air quality standards. (Courtesy of the MLC.)

Mono Lake Committee chairman David Gaines poses beside a pile of dead gull chicks in an August 2, 1981, photograph that was used to raise concern about the plight of the nesting colony and the increasing stress on the entire Mono Lake ecosystem. The primary gull nesting island, Negit, had become connected to shore in 1978 and was no longer safe from predators like coyotes, so gulls had shifted their nest activity onto smaller islets. (Courtesy of the MLC.)

"Save Mono Lake" bumper and rear window stickers became common sights on cars throughout California during the 1980s as the campaign to save Mono Lake expanded its membership. Mono Lake made the cover of *Life* and was the topic of a *National Geographic* magazine article in the 1980s. Over 20,000 people eventually became members of the Mono Lake Committee. (Courtesy of the MLC.)

David Gaines, cofounder of the Mono Lake Committee along with his wife, Sally, spent much of late 1978 through 1980 traveling across the state of California giving slide talks about the effort to save Mono Lake to Lions Clubs, Sierra Club groups, and Audubon chapter meetings. He served as a leader of the organization until his death in a car crash on January 11, 1988. (Courtesy of the MLC, photograph by Jim Stroup.)

Bikeathon and bucket walk rewatering ceremonies became annual events hosted by the Mono Lake Committee. Starting in Los Angeles at the Department of Water and Power headquarters, bicyclists filled vials of water from the fountain and then pedaled 350 miles north to return the water to Mono Lake. In Lee Vining, they joined bucket walkers who had scooped Lee Vining Creek water from above the diversion point. Together, the participants gathered at the Old Marina site on Labor Day weekends to pour their water into the lake and then participate in the Mono Lake Committee's annual meeting. (Courtesy of the MLC.)

The Mono Lake Tufa State Reserve was established in 1981 on the state owned-portions of the lake bed below the 6,417-foot elevation. An important role for the park rangers has been leading public nature walks and educational programs for local schools. Here Ranger Janet Carle demonstrates how mixing freshwater with calcium into Mono Lake's water makes tufa (the white calcium carbonate clouding the water). (Courtesy of the MLTSR.)

The Mono Basin National Forest Scenic Area was established in 1984 on the federal lands surrounding Mono Lake. The scenic area was a first of its designation for the U.S. Forest Service. The authorizing legislation also called for a major study of the lake ecosystem to be coordinated by the National Academy of Sciences and authorized $4 million for construction of a visitor center, which opened in 1992. (Courtesy of the USFS/INF.)

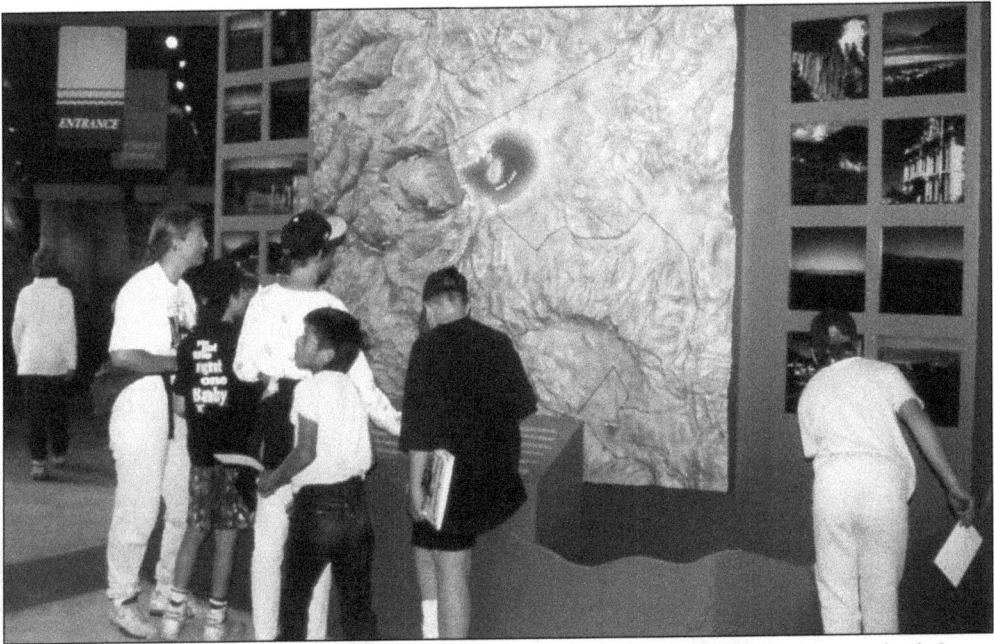

Fifth graders from Lee Vining Elementary School, with their teacher Jodie Aas on the left, try out the interactive exhibits in the Mono Basin Scenic Area Visitor Center. Each year, about 110,000 visitors come through the doors of the center, which began a partnership with Yosemite National Park in 2006, because many visitors to Mono Lake are also headed across to Yosemite. (Courtesy of the MLTSR.)

Volunteers built a boardwalk at the Old Marina site in the Mono Lake Tufa State Reserve in 1988 to help some of the quarter-of-a-million visitors that come to the lake every year walk across a section of marshy shoreline. (Courtesy of the MLTSR.)

The Old Marina boardwalk was dedicated to the memory of Mono Lake Committee cofounder David Gaines, who died in a car accident in 1988. His wife, Sally, and children, Sage and Vireo, cut the ribbon. State park ranger David Carle is on the left. (Courtesy of the MLTSR.)

The State Water Resources Control Board held a standing-room-only public hearing in Lee Vining at the Mono Basin Scenic Area Visitor Center on December 3, 1993. As part of the board's preparation for changes to the Los Angeles Department of Water and Power's water diversion licenses, they heard testimony by a panel of local old-timers about changes they had seen in recreational and scenic values at Mono Lake. From left to right are Kerry Kellogg, Bettie Shannon, Elma Blaver, and August Hess. (Courtesy of the MLC.)

On December 13, 1993, the Mono Lake Committee and the Los Angeles Department of Water and Power announced that they would jointly seek state funds for water reclamation projects and conservation projects in Los Angeles to replace water from the Mono Lake Basin. Standing before a "Save Mono Lake" banner are, from left to right, Los Angeles city councilman Nate Holden; city council president John Ferraro; Gov. Pete Wilson; Department of Water and Power general manager Dan Waters; Dennis Tito, president of the Board of Water and Power Commissioners; councilman Zeo Yaroslavsky; Los Angeles mayor Richard Riordan (at the podium); Mono Lake Committee board member Tom Soto; assemblyman Richard Katz; Mono Lake Committee executive director Martha Davis; state senator Tim Leslie; councilwoman Ruth Galanter; Marc Del Piero of the State Water Resources Control Board; and Edith and Mortimer Gaines, David's parents. (Courtesy of the MLC.)

The South Tufa Area is the most visited site at Mono Lake. Most people come during the summer months, but it is a spectacular place in all seasons. After 16 years of court decisions and appeals, protection for Mono Lake and its streams was finally announced in September 1994. The State Water Resources Control Board amended the City of Los Angeles's water diversion licenses to protect the public trust values of Mono Lake and its tributary streams. The lake is gradually filling toward the target elevation of 6,392 feet above sea level, where it will still be 25 feet below the prediversion levels but high enough to protect the ecosystem from toxic salinity levels, to maintain water around the nesting island, and to cover up enough of the exposed salt flats to control dust storms. Stream restoration measures are also underway. (Courtesy of MLTSR.)

The view from space shows how Mono Lake dominates the landscape and dwarfs other lakes and reservoirs in the nearby Eastern Sierra Nevada. This image was recorded by a satellite on December 16, 1999. (Courtesy of NASA.)

BIBLIOGRAPHY

Bean, Betty. *Horseshoe Canyon*. Bishop, CA: Chalfant Press. 1977.

Cain, Ella M. *The Story of Early Mono County*. San Francisco: Fearon Publishers. 1961.

Calhoun, Margaret. *Pioneers of Mono Basin*. Lee Vining: Robert C. Calhoun and Artemisia Press. 1984.

Carle, David. *Mono Lake Viewpoint*. Lee Vining: Artemisia Press. 1992.

Diamond, Valerie H. and Robert A. Hicks. "Historic Overview of the Rush Creek and Lee Vining Creek Hydroelectric Projects." Submitted to Southern California Edison Company by Theodoratus Cultural Research, Inc., Fair Oaks, CA, August 1988. www.monobasinresearch. org/historical/hydropowerhistory.pdf (accessed May 28, 2008).

Fletcher, Thomas C. *Paiute, Prospector, Pioneer*. Lee Vining: Artemisia Press. 1987.

Gaines, David. *Mono Lake Guidebook*. Lee Vining: Artemisia Press. 1982.

Hart, John. *Storm Over Mono, The Mono Lake Battle and the California Water Future*. Berkeley: University of California Press. 1996.

LaBraque, Lily Mathieu. *Man from Mono. A Memoir of the LaBraque Family of Mono Basin*. Reno: Nevada Academic Press. 1984.

Patera, Alan H. *Lundy*. Lake Grove, OR: Western Places. 2000.

Rose, Gene. *Yosemite's Tioga Country, A History and Appreciation*. Yosemite National Park: Yosemite Association. 2006.

Russell, Israel C. *Quaternary History of the Mono Valley, California. 8th Annual Report of the U.S. Geological Survey*. Lee Vining: Artemisia Press. 1889 (1984 reprint).

INDEX

Visit us at
arcadiapublishing.com